Prostitution

Tamara L. Roleff, Book Editor

GREENHAVEN PRESS
An imprint of Thomson Gale, a part of The Thomson Corporation

THOMSON
™
GALE

Detroit • New York • San Francisco • New Haven, Conn. • Waterville, Maine • London • Munich

Bonnie Szumski, *Publisher*
Helen Cothran, *Managing Editor*

For more information, contact:
Greenhaven Press
27500 Drake Rd.
Farmington Hills, MI 48331-3535
Or you can visit our Internet site at http://www.gale.com

LIBRARY OF CONGRESS CATALOGING-IN-PUBLICATION DATA

Prostitution / Tamara L. Roleff, book editor.
    p. cm. – (Contemporary issues companion)
    Includes bibliographical references and index.
    ISBN 0-7377-2462-5 (hardcover lib. : alk. paper) -- ISBN 0-7377-2463-3
    (pbk. : alk. paper)
    1. Prostitution. 2. Prostitution–United States. I. Roleff, Tamara L., 1959– II. Series.
    HQ111.P6992 2007
    306.740973--dc22
                                    2006016707

Printed in the United States of America
10 9 8 7 6 5 4 3 2 1

Prostitution

Other Books of Related Interest:

Opposing Viewpoints Series

Male/Female Roles

Pornography

Sex

Sexual Violence

Teenage Sexuality

Current Controversies Series

Sexual Harassment

Sexually Transmitted Diseases

Violence Against Women

At Issue Series

Child Sexual Abuse

Sex Education

Sexually Transmitted Diseases

Teen Sex

Contents

Foreword

In the news, on the streets, and in neighborhoods, individuals are confronted with a variety of social problems. Such problems may affect people directly: A young woman may struggle with depression, suspect a friend of having bulimia, or watch a loved one battle cancer. And even the issues that do not directly affect her private life—such as religious cults, domestic violence, or legalized gambling—still impact the larger society in which she lives. Discovering and analyzing the complexities of issues that encompass communal and societal realms as well as the world of personal experience is a valuable educational goal in the modern world.

Effectively addressing social problems requires familiarity with a constantly changing stream of data. Becoming well informed about today's controversies is an intricate process that often involves reading myriad primary and secondary sources, analyzing political debates, weighing various experts' opinions—even listening to firsthand accounts of those directly affected by the issue. For students and general observers, this can be a daunting task because of the sheer volume of information available in books, periodicals, on the evening news, and on the Internet. Researching the consequences of legalized gambling, for example, might entail sifting through congressional testimony on gambling's societal effects, examining private studies on Indian gaming, perusing numerous websites devoted to Internet betting, and reading essays written by lottery winners as well as interviews with recovering compulsive gamblers. Obtaining valuable information can be time-consuming—since it often requires researchers to pore over numerous documents and commentaries before discovering a source relevant to their particular investigation.

Greenhaven's Contemporary Issues Companion series seeks to assist this process of research by providing readers with useful and pertinent information about today's complex issues. Each volume in this anthology series focuses on a topic of current interest, presenting informative and thought-provoking selections written from a wide variety of viewpoints. The readings selected by the editors include such diverse sources as personal accounts and case studies, pertinent factual and statistical articles, and relevant commentaries and overviews. This diversity of sources and views, found in every Contemporary Issues Companion, offers readers a broad perspective in one convenient volume.

In addition, each title in the Contemporary Issues Companion series is designed especially for young adults. The selections included in every volume are chosen for their accessibility and are expertly edited in consideration of both the reading and comprehension levels of the audience. The structure of the anthologies also enhances accessibility. An introductory essay places each issue in context and provides helpful facts such as historical background or current statistics and legislation that pertain to the topic. The chapters that follow organize the material and focus on specific aspects of the book's topic. Every essay is introduced by a brief summary of its main points and biographical information about the author. These summaries aid in comprehension and can also serve to direct readers to material of immediate interest and need. Finally, a comprehensive index allows readers to efficiently scan and locate content.

The Contemporary Issues Companion series is an ideal launching point for research on a particular topic. Each anthology in the series is composed of readings taken from an extensive gamut of resources, including periodicals, newspapers, books, government documents, the publications of private and public organizations, and Internet websites. In these volumes, readers will find factual support suitable for use in reports, debates, speeches, and research papers. The anthologies also facilitate further research, featuring a book and periodical bibliography and a list of organizations to contact for additional information.

A perfect resource for both students and the general reader, Greenhaven's Contemporary Issues Companion series is sure to be a valued source of current, readable information on social problems that interest young adults. It is the editors' hope that readers will find the Contemporary Issues Companion series useful as a starting point to formulate their own opinions about and answers to the complex issues of the present day.

Introduction

Society's attitude toward prostitution have changed dramatically over the millennia. The earliest prostitutes were actually temple priestesses in Mesopotamia who were revered and honored for their religious service. The sex rituals of the priestesses-prostitutes were a sacred means for men—kings and commoners alike—to commune with the gods and goddesses and discern their will. Some sexual encounters took the form of a fertility ritual. The temple prostitutes also performed important public services. For example, in the four-thousand-year-old Babylonian *Epic of Gilgamesh*, which contains the Western world's first written reference to a prostitute, the temple priestess spends six days and seven nights with Enkidu, a strong, hairy savage. During their time together the prostitute teaches Enkidu about love, tenderness, and sex, as well as how to eat and drink and how to clean and take care of himself. In short, she civilizes him before she sends him back out into the world.

In the fifth century B.C., the Greek historian Herodotus wrote about the sacred prostitutes of Ishtar, the Babylonian goddess of love and war who is called the Whore of Babylon in the Bible. According to Herodotus,

> Babylonian custom . . . compels every woman of the land once in her life to sit in the temple of love and have intercourse with some stranger. . . . The men pass and make their choice. It matters not what be the sum of money; the woman will never refuse, for that were a sin, the money being by this act made sacred. After their intercourse she has made herself holy in the sight of the goddess and goes away to her home.

With the rise of monotheism, views of prostitution began to change from one in which female prostitutes were revered as sacred and as fertility symbols to one in which they were manifestations of evil who lured men into sin. The Bible mentions prostitutes numerous times. Jezebel is probably the most notorious prostitute in the Old Testament. As queen of Israel, she was the high priestess for the god Baal and his consort Ashera, who were worshipped by licentious living, sensual dancing, and sex. Jezebel was especially reviled by the Israelites because she was intolerant of the Jews' god, Yahweh, and she tried to convert the Israelites to her pagan beliefs. Eventually, she led a religious war against the Israelites and their god. She met a tragic end, however, when she was pushed out a window. To the Israelites, it was a fitting punishment for one who worshipped carnal pleasure.

In the fourth century A.D. the Christian theologian and philosopher Augustine of Hippo wrote his *Confessions*, in which he describes his conversion to Christianity and denounces the wildness of his youth, which included numerous encounters with prostitutes. Despite his new attitude toward sinful living, Augustine continued to support the practice of prostitution, explaining, "If you expel prostitution from society, you will unsettle everything on account of lusts." Thomas Aquinas, a thirteenth-century philosopher and theologian, believed lust was a mortal sin, and that prostitution was "filthy," "unlawful," "shameful," "venal," and "against the law of God." Nevertheless, Aquinas agreed with Augustine that prostitution should be tolerated. In her book *Mary Magdalene: Myth and Metaphor*, Susan Haskins explains Aquinas's contradictory views. She says that for Aquinas, "prostitution had the function of a sewer within a palace which, if it were removed, would leave the palace filled with pollution. Similarly, if it [prostitution] were eliminated, the world would be filled with sodomy, which would be infinitely more heinous." Augustine and Aquinas therefore believed that prostitution, however sinful, must be endured to prevent lustful men from seducing or raping virtuous women or each other. This paradox—allowing prostitution while at the same time condemning it—remained a consistent, if awkward, part of public policy for the next several hundred years.

Prostitution continued to be viewed as a necessary evil through the Middle Ages and Renaissance, and prostitutes were generally left alone to ply their trade as long as they did not bother "respectable" people. In fact, during the Renaissance many European cities attempted to regulate prostitution by requiring prostitutes to wear distinctive clothing or hats that immediately identified their profession. In the eighteenth and nineteenth centuries, however, sexually transmitted diseases—specifically syphilis—became a serious problem among prostitutes and their clients, and European countries began earnestly trying to control prostitution. Brothels (houses of prostitution) were closed, and some cities initiated mandatory health examinations for prostitutes. Ultimately, stricter punishments were enacted for those caught selling sex. Sex trafficking, known then as "the white slave trade," also became a problem at this time; people were shocked to discover that women and girls were shipped across international borders and forced into prostitution. During the late nineteenth and early twentieth centuries, the United States, Great Britain, and other European countries passed laws forbidding sex trafficking and established agencies to deal with the problem.

As in Europe, prostitution was legal in most areas of the United States until the early twentieth century. Where it was not legal, polite society either ignored it, or law enforcement was bribed to look the other way. In the Wild West, prostitution was generally allowed, but some sheriffs imposed their own rules to control it. Doc Linton, the sheriff of Tombstone, Arizona, posted a notice in 1882 advising the town's prostitutes to behave themselves:

> All women of dubious character in the fair city of Tombstone must continue to confine themselves to the shady side of the street. . . . You all know who this concerns. If any of

you are seen on the sunny side of the street, there's a quiet place waiting for you—jail. The alternative is to leave town for good. At any rate, that would be good for Tombstone.

"Virtuous" women were hard to find in the Wild West, where the men outnumbered women by at least five to one. It is estimated that 10 percent of women in the Wild West were prostitutes, with 25 percent of those being former slaves who were freed by the Civil War. These women were quite different from the settlers' and ranchers' wives, teachers, and missionaries who came west during the 1800s, and it was not often that their paths would cross. Prostitutes during the time of the Wild West could be found in brothels, saloons, dance halls, and laundries—businesses that few respectable women would patronize. Many prostitutes married their customers, thereby attaining instant respectability. But the majority simply endured, facing social derision, ill-tempered clients, and the possibility of death at the hands of an unstable or drunk client.

A concerted effort was made at the turn of the twentieth century to outlaw prostitution. The Women's Christian Temperance Union (WCTU)—originally formed in the late 1870s to rid America of the problem of alcohol abuse—was influential in criminalizing prostitution as another social ill. Prevailing attitudes of the time held that prostitutes had weaker morals than men, which explained why some women "succumbed" to such a disrespectful lifestyle. In addition, various ethnic immigrant women were believed to be "dirty" and were therefore more likely to become prostitutes. Between 1910 and 1920 the WCTU succeeded in its lobbying efforts to make prostitution illegal in almost every state. These laws remain in place to this day. Nevada is the only state where prostitution has been kept legal in some counties.

Modern-day attitudes toward prostitution vary between those that treat prostitutes as women who were forced into the profession and need help to leave it (prostitute as exploited victim) and those that view prostitutes as immoral and unworthy of legal protections (prostitute as promiscuous woman). In either case women are stigmatized by society if their work as a prostitute becomes known. Male prostitutes, if they are thought of at all, do not face the same problems as female prostitutes. Male prostitutes are rarely arrested nor do they share the stigma that attaches to women prostitutes.

Laws and attitudes regarding "johns"—the male customers of prostitutes—are just as conflicting. Johns are breaking the law by soliciting sex, but traditionally they have not been targeted for arrest. If they are arrested, their punishment generally amounts to a small fine. Since the 1990s some cities have been slowly changing their public policy concerning prostitution. Under the theory that the only way to eradicate prostitution is to eliminate the demand for it, law enforcement in cities such as Chicago, Cincinnati, and Vancouver, Canada, are now targeting the customers instead of the prostitutes. Police are arresting more and more johns, confiscating their cars, and displaying the men's photos on city police Web sites. Johns are also being encouraged to attend classes in which they are educated about how prostitution affects both women and men.

The reasons why women prostitute themselves are many and complex. Despite changes in society's perceptions of prostitution and the legality of the profession, it remains prevalent around the world. To this end, *Prostitution: Contemporary Issues Companion* offers an overview of various aspects of this important social issue. The authors included in this volume explore the world of prostitution, examine proposed legal remedies and their effectiveness, and offer several personal perspectives on prostitution.

CHAPTER 1

Defining Prostitution

Sex for Money Is Not Always Prostitution

Marc Perkel

Marc Perkel hosts a Web site on sex and prostitution. The following selection is a legal brief Perkel wrote for escort services, advising them on when paid sexual activity is considered prostitution. According to Perkel's argument, there are many instances when money or some other item of value changes hands and sex occurs, but these examples do not meet the legal definition of prostitution. For example, Perkel notes that pornography, lap dancing, buying gifts for a date, and sex therapy all may include an exchange of money and sex, but they are not defined as prostitution. Perkel concludes that sex for money is prostitution only when there is no other element involved in the transaction.

What is prostitution? Is an escort service a prostitution business? Are all instances of sex for money prostitution? Are all exchanges of sex for money illegal? If not, what differentiates legal sex for money and illegal sex for money? What are the moral and ethical issues involving prostitution, sex, and money and where does the law fit in? What are the rights of the individual to have sexual intercourse and what rights does society have to control the sexual behavior of consenting adults? These are the questions I am going to attempt to answer here in an attempt to create legal arguments that I hope will be instructive to courts, judges, prosecutors, and defense lawyers in the battle over the role the government has in regulating the exchange of money for sexual contact. . . .

Marc Perkel, "Escort Services Legal Issues," sex.perkel.com. Reproduced by permission of the author.

Legal Definitions of Prostitution

The laws defining and controlling prostitution vary from state to state. I live in Missouri and prostitution and other important legal concepts are defined by Missouri Statute 567-010 as follows:

"Prostitution", a person commits prostitution if he engages or offers or agrees to engage in sexual conduct with another person in return for something of value to be received by the person or by a third person. . . .

Sex and Money

Other than breathing and eating, people spend much of their time involved in reproductive activities or making and spending money. Sex is everywhere. If we aren't having intercourse, we're thinking about having intercourse. Much time and effort is spent trying to or preparing for intercourse. Men and women both spend a lot of time and money to have sex. We buy clothes to look good to the opposite sex and to send messages to keep sexual competitors at bay. We put on chemicals that smell good and stimulate a sexual response in the person we are trying to attract. Men work to make money to buy a house and to accumulate money and security to attract women so that there is a stable enough environment for a woman to feel comfortable to have children.

Women know instinctively to be attracted to men who are capable of not only producing quality genetic material, but to show that he can be a source of food, clothing, and shelter so as to raise children to reproductive age. It is human nature for a male to demonstrate his ability to be a resource to the female so as to get her to consider him as a possibility to father her children. Thus sex and money are closely related.

In the animal kingdom the strongest males drive off other males and defend the .females and offspring from predators. Human females are similar in that females who carefully select their males on the basis of being able to sustain a family have reproduced more successfully than females who were less discriminating. Thus women have evolved to want men with money. And men have evolved to make money as a means of attracting women. Sex and money have a biological connection.

Men and women both spend huge amounts of money to make themselves more attractive. Why do men and women wear false hair pieces? Because it visually stimulates potential sex partners. Why do women get breast implants? The reason is not to enhance the feeding of babies. These implants are to make themselves more sexually desirable to men. One only has to look at the amount of money spent on clothing, perfumes, makeup, and Viagra to see that people are willing to spend a great deal of money in order to get sexual contact. So if it is moral to spend huge amounts to get the chance to have sex, then it seems to follow that some people are likely to spend money directly to have sex.

Having sex, thinking about having sex, and preparing to have sex involves a lot of the average person's time in the average day. People also spend a lot of time earning a living, making money, spending money, or saving money. There is also a lot of time and money spent in relation to having sex. Families are very expensive. Raising kids and educating them is all part of sexual reproduction. With so much of humanity involved in money and sex, there are going to be a huge number of transactions that involve both money and sex at the same time. In fact, there are probably very few sexual encounters where money isn't somehow involved. Even marriage, the most widely accepted form of sexual union, is in legal terms a contract in which the two parties merge their property. In a relationship without children, a marriage contract is really a property contract in the eyes of the courts.

Sex, Money, and Prostitution

If prostitution is sex for money and money plays a part in most sex acts, then is most sex really prostitution? If prostitution were defined that simply, the answer would be Yes. But we all know that's not the case. Prostitution isn't just the union of sex and money, which occurs all the time, it's specifically sex for money. For an act to be prostitution there has to be an understanding that the person is paying money to have sex. That narrows it down a lot.

Thus if a man buys a woman flowers and chocolates in hopes that she will have intercourse, or a woman cooks dinner for a man hoping for sexual contact, that's not prostitution. Even if a man gives a woman money as a gift because he is expecting or hoping for sexual contact in exchange for the gift, that's not prostitution. So there is a lot of cases where people spend money to get sex that is not prostitution because it lacks a specific agreement to have sex in exchange for "something of value".

Under Missouri law the definition of "something of value" is interesting in that it is defined as something exchangeable for money or property. It doesn't define services as something of value, especially services that don't produce a product that can be exchanged for money or property. Thus, the way I read Missouri law, a woman can have sex with her lawyer in exchange for legal services because legal services don't fit the definition of "something of value" as defined by statute. If a woman offered sex to a man for fixing her car, that might go either way based on the idea that maintenance could be construed as increasing the resale value of the car. If a woman traded sex for a man managing a stock portfolio, it would only be prostitution if he made money in the market.

Is Sex for Money Always Prostitution?

Although the law defines prostitution as basically sex for money, this rule doesn't always apply. There are many cases where people are paid money or "something of value" in exchange for sexual contact and it is not prostitution. It seems logical at this point to list examples of sex for money that is not prostitution in order to more accurately develop a set of rules to determine what prostitution is by examining what it is not.

For example, the making of a porn movie is not prostitution. But in a porn movie you have sexual contact and the actors are paid to have sex in front of a camera. This is clearly sex for money, but it's not prostitution.

We have all seen movies involving love making on the screen. Many sex scenes have even made it to prime time television. They involve simulated sex. Simulated sex is where the actors don't have genital penetration. The visuals are often faked, although in many cases, real sexual stimulation occurs. Although much of the sex is simulated sex, often the scene involves the licking of nipples, grinding of groins, kissing of the thighs and navels, penises get hard, faces get red, nipples become erect. These acts are real and these people are doing it for money. Is this prostitution? No! Is this sex for money? Yes it is. But, they're making a movie. Thus it is legal to have sex for money in the context of making a movie.

A man goes into a topless bar and sits down next to the stage. He pulls out a dollar bill, folds it lengthwise and lays it on the stage. The female dancer sees the money and moves right in front of him. She shakes her breasts in his face, spreads her legs, shows him her ass and moves her hips in a humping motion. She then turns and kisses him on the forehead and pulls her garter indicating for him to put the money there. He does, and she repeats the performance for the next man with a dollar. Is this prostitution? No. Is it sex for money? Yes it is. But it's dancing.

A woman is working for a large company. Her supervisor is a handsome single man. An opportunity for a promotion opens up. She indicates to her supervisor that she's willing to have sex with him if she gets the job. The new job pays more than her present job. They have known each other for years and have dated in the past but never had sex. She has sex with him and she gets the job. Is it unethical? Yes it is. Is it sex for money? Yes it is. Is it prostitution? No.

A man and a woman are dating. They are out shopping and she sees something she wants. He asks if he buys the item for her if she'll have sex with him. She agrees. Is that prostitution? No. Is it sex for money? Yes it is. But it's in the context of a relationship. It may be a screwed-up relationship, but it's not a crime. We are Americans and we have the right to have a screwed-up relationship.

A couple is having sexual problems. Their marriage is in a rut and they are talking about divorce. The problem is that the "spark" is gone. Sex just isn't good any more. That may be a bad reason to divorce, but it happens. In an attempt to save the relationship, they go to a sexual counselor. The counselor examines the couple and determines that they need training in sexual technique. This training is to be accomplished by sexual surrogates. The couple is taken to a room where a staff male and a staff female engage in sexual intercourse with the couple and train them in sexual techniques. The staff members are total strangers and are having sex with the couple for money. Is this prostitution? No! Is it sex for money? Yes it is. But it is in the context of therapy. Even if the sexual surrogates are not licensed or trained it's not prostitution. It is at best a license violation.

A smart young man has an affair with a rich old woman. She is lonely and she desperately wants sexual contact. He lives with her and takes care of her needs. She takes care of his expenses. Both know what's going on. He knows if he doesn't give her sex that he's gone. She knows that if she doesn't give him money he's gone. However, they have lived together for a long time and are both getting what they want. Is this prostitution? No. Is it sex for money? Yes it is. A prosecutor might in theory be able to press criminal charges, but what jury would actually convict either party of prostitution, especially if there were other things that they did together besides sex and money. . . .

What Makes Sex for Money Not Prostitution?

We have now listed several examples of sex for money that is not prostitution. What is the common element that makes sex for money not prostitution? If you are making a movie then sex for money isn't prostitution. If it is part of dancing on stage then sex for money isn't prostitution. If it's in the context of a relationship then sex for money isn't prostitution. If it's in the context of therapy then sex for money isn't prostitution. If it's in the context of getting a job then sex for money isn't prostitution. If it's in the context of friendship then sex for money isn't prostitution. If they are living together then sex for money isn't prostitution.

It seems that the common element that makes sex for money not prostitution is that if it's not only sex for money. In all these cases there is a third element involved. It's always sex for money and something else. The one example of prostitution was when there was only sex for money and nothing else. Thus, although the statute defines prostitution as sexual contact in exchange for something of value, it seems like in practice that the real rule is an exchange of something of value for only sex and nothing else. Because if you are buying sex and friendship or sex in the context of a relationship or therapy, or making a movie, then the third element makes the event not an act of prostitution, even with the element of sex for money.

Thus the language of the statute is incomplete because it doesn't say what it really means. Prostitution is more accurately defined as:

"Prostitution", a person commits prostitution if he, in return for something of value to be received by the person or by a third person, engages or offers or agrees to engage in *only* sexual conduct with another person.

Why Pornography Is Not Legally Defined as Prostitution

Sherry F. Colb

In the following article Sherry F. Colb discusses a court case in which a judge ruled that makers of adult films were not practicing prostitution. Prostitution is defined as paying money to someone for sex; pornography involves a customer paying money to watch other people have sex without the viewer participating in the sex acts. Colb attests that there is a fine line between paying money to watch other people have sex and paying money to have sex oneself; however, the courts have maintained that pornography is not prostitution and is protected by the First Amendment right to free speech. Colb is a professor and the Frederick B. Lacey Scholar at Rutgers Law School in Newark, New Jersey, and a columnist for FindLaw, an online legal information site.

Jenny Paulino stands accused of running a prostitution ring on the Upper East Side of Manhattan. Among other defense arguments, Paulino moved to dismiss the case on Equal Protection grounds. She claimed that the Manhattan District Attorney's office selectively targets "escort services" for prosecution, while ignoring distributors of adult films, who are engaged in what is essentially the same activity.

Justice Budd G. Goodman . . . issued a ruling rejecting Paulino's claim, on the ground that pornography does not qualify as prostitution under the relevant New York statute. "[P]rostitution," said Justice Goodman, "is and has always been intuitively defined as a bilateral exchange between a prostitute and a client." Therefore, the judge explained, the District Attorney's office has *not* ignored one form of prostitution and pursued another, within the meaning of the law.

Sherry F. Colb, "Is Pornography the Same as Prostitution?," FindLaw.com, August 10, 2005. Reproduced by permission.

Though the Equal Protection argument may be weak as a matter of statutory interpretation, the distinction between prostitution and pornography is not nearly as clear as Justice Goodman suggests.

What Is Prostitution?

As Justice Goodman asserts, most of us typically think of prostitution as involving a customer who pays a prostitute for providing sexual services to that customer. We intuit that pornography, by contrast, involves a customer paying an actor for providing sexual services to another actor.

In other words, prostitution is generally understood as the bilateral trading of sex for money, while pornography involves the customer of an adult film paying money to watch other people have sex with each other, while receiving no sexual favors himself in return for his money.

In keeping with this distinction, notes Justice Goodman, "the pornographic motion picture industry has flourished without prosecution since its infancy." The failure of the New York legislature to do anything about this state of affairs, moreover, further demonstrates that New York's prostitution statute was never intended to encompass pornography.

Is It Sensible to Exclude Pornography from Laws Against Prostitution?

Justice Goodman may be correct about the statute in question, although the statutory language does not help his position.

New York Penal Law defines a prostitute as a person "who engages or agrees or offers to engage in sexual conduct with another person in return for a fee." A pornographic actor does just that: Like a more typical prostitute, he or she engages in sex in return for a fee.

Still, as Justice Goodman points out, traditional interpretations of the word "prostitute" narrow the literal definition to exempt pornography.

But that leads to another question: Does the pornography exemption make sense?

Stated differently, the District Attorney's office has perhaps correctly divined the legislative intent behind the statute at issue, but there might nonetheless be something fundamentally unfair about exempting distributors of nonobscene pornography from the vice laws.

To appreciate the unfairness, let us examine some of the arguments *for* this distinction.

Free Speech: One Possible Distinction between Prostitution and Pornography

Most distributors of pornography would express shock at the prospect of being prosecuted for promoting prostitution. Under *Miller v. California*, as long as a work, taken as a whole, has "serious literary, artistic, political, or scientific value," the First Amendment protects its distribution. Given this legal principle, how could pornography be criminal, in the way that prostitution is?

One might begin to formulate an answer in the following way. The process of filming and distributing pornography is indeed considered protected speech, under the Supreme Court's First Amendment precedents. However, the First Amendment does not insulate the commission of crime from prosecution just because someone with a camera records the crime and intends to sell that recording to customers.

In keeping with this portrayal, one could reasonably characterize pornography as the payment of prostitutes for having sex in front of a camera. Though the film itself might be protected by the First Amendment, it could nonetheless constitute evidence of paid-for sexual encounters—that is, evidence of prostitution—if a statute were designed to extend to that sort of prostitution.

For clarification, let us take an example from another area of criminal law. Doug the drug-dealer sells Carl the customer

Strip bars and peep shows are not considered the same as prostitution because patrons are paying to watch sexual acts, not participate in them, and this is protected free speech, according to the First Amendment. © Barry Lewis/Corbis.

eight ounces of marijuana. Both Doug and Carl are guilty of (different) criminal acts for having engaged in this illicit transaction. Assume that there is an audience for such transactions on reality television (all rights reserved). In anticipation of this audience, Fiona the filmmaker pays Doug and Carl to permit her to tape them carrying out their business.

Has Fiona done anything illegal? No, but neither has her First-Amendment-protected act of filming and distributing her recording altered the illegal character of Doug's and Carl's conduct. Doug and Carl may still be prosecuted for engaging in a drug transaction, despite the fact that Fiona may not be prosecuted for taping it or showing the tape.

Furthermore, Fiona's tape may be subpoenaed and used by the District Attorney's office as evidence of the drug transactions charged against Doug and Carl.

Some Possible Differences Between Filming Drug-Dealing and Filming Pornography

To be sure, there are some differences between Fiona and the pornography distributor, which might translate into differences between pornographic actors, on the one hand, and Doug and Carl, on the other.

In our example, Doug and Carl have engaged in a drug transaction, and the only element that Fiona has added to the mix is her filming of that transaction. In the case of pornography, however, the actors having sex are doing so precisely *because* they are being filmed. The taping, in other words, is not just "evidence" of their having sex; it is the entire point of that sex. In pornography, then, the recording is an integral, rather than a peripheral, part of the transaction.

What this means is that unlike Doug and Carl, the people who have sex for the camera are actors, and acting—unlike drug-dealing or prostitution—is part of what falls within the protection of the First Amendment.

A better analogy to pornography might therefore be a film-maker paying Doug and Carl to *act* as though they are dealing drugs for the camera when in fact they are not. In such a case, of course, there would be no grounds for prosecuting the two men.

Not So Fast: Does the Pornographic Actor/ Prostitute Distinction Really Work?

The distinction between pornography and prostitution is not, however, quite so straightforward as the latter analogy suggests. A couple having *actual* sex for the camera—let's call the people Jason and June—is different from Doug and Carl *pretending* to deal drugs. Doug and Carl really are just acting, but having intercourse is not just acting—it is also bona fide sex.

That is what distinguishes a pornographic film from a film in which people pretend that they're having sex when they are not. In that sense, the reality TV example of Doug and Carl may be more like adult film than it initially appeared to be. Doug and Carl truly *are* dealing drugs and there is also filming going on, just as Jason and June really *are* having sex and there is also filming going on.

Why Real Sex is Not like Acting, from the Law's Point of View

But why should the distinction between pretending to have sex, and actually having it, make a difference, from a legal standpoint?

The sex act is a legally significant event. If it occurs without consent, it is rape. If it takes place between a married person and a third party, it is adultery. If it occurs and leads to the birth of a child, then the man is legally responsible for that child until the age of 18. And if it happens in exchange for a fee, then it is prostitution.

Pretending to have sex, however, for a camera or in private, triggers none of these legal consequences and can therefore be characterized as mere acting.

Who Is Paying Whom and Should It Matter?

When pornography is correctly understood as involving real sex, the question in comparing pornography to prostitution becomes whether *who is paying whom* matters (or should matter) to the law. That is, should it make a difference whether Jason pays June to have sex with Jason or whether, instead, Filmore (the filmmaker) pays June to have sex with Jason?

If these two scenarios seem functionally equivalent, then there may be something seriously wrong with our laws.

Consider the following example. Jason has just turned 21, and he is a virgin. His uncle Lecher believes that Jason should have some experience with sex before he finishes college, so Lecher pays June (a family friend) to have sex with Jason. Jason happily accepts this gift, and June carries out her side of the deal.

It does seem that in this example, prostitution has taken place. The payor may not be the same person as the recipient of sexual services, but so what? In all relevant respects, this transaction appears to fall within any reasonable definition of prostitution, with June in the role of prostitute and either Lecher or Jason or both (depending on the state of mind of each of them with respect to the quid pro quo [exchange]) in the role of customer. Justice Goodman's emphasis on the bilateral nature of prostitution no longer seems well-placed.

How Are Adult Films Different?

If it "intuitively" seems like prostitution even when a third party pays someone to have sex with another third party, then what makes adult films so different? Is it the fact that Uncle Lecher is not seeking his own sexual gratification (in the way that a customer of pornography is) but someone else's (Jason's)? If so, then assume that Uncle Lecher wants to watch June and Jason having sex. That added feature hardly seems to mitigate the character of the act as prostitution.

Is the important difference instead the fact that Jason, the college student, is seeking sexual gratification from June, the prostitute, while neither Jason the porn star nor June the porn star are seeking sexual gratification for themselves? If that matters, then assume that Jason the porn star loves his work (and could be earning a lot more as a regular actor), so he is as interested in sexual gratification as Jason the college student is.

On these facts, in both pornography and conventional prostitution, people are having sex with other people as a condition of getting paid, and someone seeking sexual gratification but not money is ultimately driving the demand for the activity (the customer of the prostitute, in one case, and the future viewer of the pornography, on the other).

The First Amendment Returns: Why the Court Protects Pornographic Films

Having said all of this, it is nonetheless almost certain that on its current precedents, the U.S. Supreme Court would hold that garden-variety pornographic actors are indeed engaged in First-Amendment-protected activity, so long as obscenity—as defined by the *Miller* test, quoted in part above—is not involved. Odd as it may seem, what appears finally to make all of the difference is the mode of gratification for the person who is paying but not himself seeking money.

The ultimate demand for pornography comes from the viewer of pornography, and what excites him is the watching of the adult film, rather than any physical act performed on him by another person. The "enjoyment" of pornography is therefore as "speech," rather than as action.

Though real sex occurred in the making of the pornographic film, this fact is only relevant insofar as it is known (or believed) by the viewer. If, for example, the entire film were created with highly realistic computer graphics, but the viewer believed that what he saw was real, then he would enjoy the material just as much.

Because the impact of pornography occurs through the mediation of an audience witnessing a performance, rather than an audience receiving physical services from a performer, pornography and its making qualify as First-Amendment protected speech.

Does this make sense? Consider again the significance of the sexual act: legal consequences can follow from it and it can, accordingly, be regulated by the law in a variety of ways. Though two people may very much want to have sex with each other in private, the law can intervene to say that they cannot, just because one of them seeks money and the other gratification, for example.

If, however, both members of the couple are in it for the money, and there is a man with a camera taping them so that millions of people can buy or rent the tape and masturbate to it, then the sex is insulated by the Constitution from legal regulation.

That is in fact the law, but Jenny Paulino can hardly be faulted for calling it arbitrary.

Is Prostitution Forced Oppression or a Chosen Lifestyle?

Katia Dunn

Katia Dunn is a reporter for the Portland, Oregon, Mercury News. In the following article Dunn writes about three organizations that attempt to help prostitutes. She notes that each of these organizations views prostitution in a different manner. One organization, LOTUS, is run by social workers who see prostitutes as an oppressed class—victims of their race and poverty. The prostitutes who use the services of LOTUS often want to leave prostitution. The second organization, Danzine, is run by current and former sex workers who try to provide prostitutes with whatever they need to do their job safely, such as condoms and clean needles. According to Dunn, Danzine employees view prostitution as a chosen lifestyle. The last organization, COYOTE, is a national prostitutes' union that advocates for the legalization of sex work. COYOTE argues that prostitutes should have more rights and should not be labeled as mere criminals.

Melissa Farley, a clinical and research psychologist, is one of the nation's leading researchers on prostitution. According to her 1998 study of 475 prostitutes from five different countries—including women, men, and transgendered individuals—62 percent of prostitutes reported having been raped in prostitution, 73 percent reported having experienced physical assault in prostitution, 72 percent were currently or formerly homeless, and 92 percent stated they wanted to escape prostitution immediately.

Katia Dunn, "Prostitution: Pro or Con?," *Portland Mercury News*, May 9–15, 2002. Reproduced by permission.

Helping Women Escape Prostitution

Nikki Williams is a caseworker at the Portland [Oregon]-based organization LOTUS, which stands for "Liberating Ourselves Through Understanding Sexploitation," a government-funded program aimed at helping women escape prostitution, and she knows the stories of the women those numbers reflect. In Nikki's life, she has met thousands of prostitutes.

"The situation that really bothered me, the woman I'll never forget, was a woman I met when I was doing outreach into a prison," says Nikki. "The woman disclosed it was her 20th birthday. She had two kids currently in SCF [Services to Children and Families] custody, and had been in and out of prison her entire life. She was turned out when she was 10 by her parents, who shot her up with cocaine because she was nervous about turning her first trick."

Nikki's eyes water as she talks about it.

"She was 20, but she looked about 14," she explains. "I saw her a year later—she was in another prison—and she looked about 55," she explained. "She's still in jail today. She was made a drug-addicted, prostituted woman at 10, and has been all her life. Where was her choice in being made a prostituted woman?"

Nikki and another case manager at LOTUS, Swana Thompson, work in the small upstairs of a building off NE 39th and Sandy. Their space is clean and peaceful, designed to be a "safe space" for the women they serve, who are largely minorities. The clients who come to them are always involved in prostitution, often referred by the courts because they have been cycling in and out of the justice system for so long, and sometimes hear about LOTUS by word of mouth.

"We've had women run in here black and blue with bruises—literally running for their lives from their pimps," Nikki explained.

In Portland, the "prostitution-free" zones—which city government argues are in place to prevent illegal sex—seem to only facilitate the easier arrest of prostitutes. According to Nikki, if a previously convicted prostitute is even *seen* by police in a prostitution-free zone—which includes areas of 82nd, Sandy, and Burnside—they are immediately arrested. LOTUS is located right in the middle of a prostitution-free zone. Consequently, women are often too scared to even come close.

Prostitution as Oppression

The principal belief driving the people at LOTUS is that prostitution and all other forms of sex work are oppression. In fact, Nikki doesn't even like to use the term "sex work," believing it suggests that prostitutes might enjoy being prostitutes. She prefers, instead, to think of all forms of sex work as prostitution.

"Some people are prostituted at places like strip clubs and brothels, places where prostitution is legal, and what they don't seem to realize is that the guy they're giving their money to, that club owner, the bouncer, the bar tender, or manager, is their pimp. He's just a corporate pimp, not a street-level pimp."

At LOTUS, the work isn't easy. The list of afflictions women suffer from after years of prostitution is long: post-traumatic stress disorder, bi-polar disorder, schizophrenia. Swana and Nikki want to help, but sometimes the women disclose information that social workers are legally bound to tell the police—like if they're selling their children. One time, Swana says, she admitted a woman, found her housing, and then the next day, the woman died. Even when things go well, the resources at LOTUS are slim.

"One time, I got this woman all set up, found her a house and everything," says Swana. "And she said to me, 'Swana, I'm living in the exact same situation I was living in before. I'm living with a slum lord. People have given me the clothes they don't want.'"

Often, landlords know when tenants are former prostitutes and give them the worst apartment in the building or try to take advantage of them, figuring they won't mind because they're used to it. A large part of the time, the women who come to them are also suffering from drug addiction.

"Prostitution and drug addiction go hand in hand," Nikki explains. "Unfortunately, people seem to believe the myth that prostituted women prostitute for the sake of the drugs. However, in the beginning, the drugs are taken to numb the effects of prostitution and in the end, the drugs take over. Sometimes, even after they get clean and go off the drugs, they will relapse into prostitution because they need money. Once they relapse into prostitution, they relapse into drug abuse. This is an endless cycle."

Overwhelmingly, the women LOTUS works with want to get out of prostitution. Often, they've been in it since before the age of 15 and have been conditioned not to know any other way of working or making money.

"People don't understand," says Nikki, "that the pimp is usually the 'boyfriend,' the 'husband,' or the 'baby daddy'. He's sitting at home while she's out being prostituted."

"Prostitution is not work. It's more than just a sexual act." Nikki explains. "It's a degradation of your spirit, a sacrifice of the soul, and abuse of the body and spirit. It is slavery."

The Race Issue

Occasionally, Nikki is invited to speak at colleges to women's studies classes about issues of prostitution.

"The women that I do community education to are usually surprised," Nikki explains, "because the mostly white, educated, upper-class audience doesn't seem to understand the racism involved in prostitution. They don't seem to understand that even under these circumstances, there is the privilege of having white skin."

"If you're white and educated, you might see stripping as an option, but if you're poor, a woman of color, drug-addicted, or were turned out into the trade when you were 12, it's not an option. Your choice has been taken."

Statistics do indicate that, overwhelmingly, the majority of prostitutes come from abused families and are abused on the job. In 1991, the local Council for Prostitution Alternatives stated that 85 percent of prostitutes reported history of sexual abuse in childhood and 70 percent reported incest. The same report indicated that "78 percent of women who sought help from the Council for Prostitution Alternatives in 1991 reported being raped an average of 16 times a year by pimps, and were raped 33 times a year by John[s]." Another study, conducted in 1994 by the Council for Prostitution Alternatives in Portland, reported that 85 percent of prostitutes are raped by pimps.

Melissa Farley, who, aside from being a leading researcher on the topic, is also working to compile one of the more comprehensive websites on prostitution research (prostitutionresearch.com), believes that not only are oppressed minorities most often the victims of prostitution, but they are also in the largest demand.

"You cannot understand prostitution unless you understand how sex, class, and race all come together and hurt a person at the same time," she explains. "People are chosen in prostitution because of the extreme imbalance of power."

"The poorest, the most vulnerable women are basically made available for constant sexual access," she explains. According to Farley, people who hire prostitutes seek out the most helpless victims in order to exploit the imbalance of power.

Danzine

Across town from LOTUS . . . is the headquarters of Danzine, located in the back of their non-profit thrift store, Miss Mona's

Rack. The shelves in the back of the store are stocked with boxes of needles, condoms, and files organized by categories of sexually transmitted diseases. There is a sign on the wall that reads, "f**k safe, shoot clean," as well as slick pictures of exotic dancers wearing lingerie. Danzine's mission statement reads, "It is our goal to share the resources and information we need to make informed decisions, personally and professionally."

Unlike the people at LOTUS, the people involved in Danzine almost always use the term "sex work" over prostitution and, also unlike LOTUS, do not advocate that prostitution is necessarily a system of oppression. Aside from running the store and the non-profit organization, Danzine has ventured into looking at sex work as an art form by organizing a publication and a biannual film festival—both put together by sex workers.

"I wouldn't say sex work is good or bad," says Teresa Dulce, director and founder of Danzine. "It's more like sex work just *is*, like the way the ocean swims and the night falls. The moment you have some kind of civilization, you're going to have currency and trade."

Therefore, Danzine tries to give sex workers whatever they need, in the moment they need it, rather than attempting to pull them out of prostitution in the long-term. Whether that means facilitating sex work or not is irrelevant. It is respected as the woman's choice and her ability to be self-reliant.

Another major difference between Danzine and LOTUS is that, while LOTUS is run by social workers, Danzine is run "by and for sex workers." According to their flyer, "dancers, models, escorts, working girls, phone operators, fetish specialists, adult entertainers, people under 18, survivors, internet players, and more are invited to contribute their words, action, and art work in *danzine*, the publication, and agency programs."

"We are the people we serve," explains Teresa. "We don't use the word 'client.'"

There is the distinct feeling, inside Danzine, that the conditions of prostitution and sex work can be made better by making informed, educated decisions and by taking control of the situation. It's a foregone conclusion that the choice to do sex work is in the hands of the sex worker.

COYOTE

Carol Leigh is the media representative for a national alliance of sex workers, called COYOTE, and has been working in the sex industry since 1977. She started in a massage parlor, worked in networks of call girls, and is currently teaching film in San Francisco. She also works at St. James Infirmary, a clinic that serves the sex industry, and has just returned from the "Sex Work and Health in a Changing Europe" conference in London, which was attended by 400 people.

"I'm not really in prostitution full-time anymore," she explains. "I mean, I have a few regulars who call me once in a while. . . ."

While Carol certainly agrees that racism is widespread in the sex industry, she believes that one solution to ending racism—both in the sex industry and in the world—is to help prostitutes become less marginalized through labor laws and legalization of prostitution.

"I don't want to be simplistic," she explains, "it's not like we can just say, 'okay let's make a union,' but in my perspective, sex workers of color need more support for voicing their terms and their issues."

Carol objects to Farley's research because she believes it limits the ways in which people understand prostitution. "Melissa researches those who are in marginalized situations," Carol explains. "She basically tries to define prostitution through statistics and descriptions of prostitutes in the most marginalized circumstances, which of course represents prostitution from the perspective of her position."

Though Carol doesn't have any numbers to counter those of Farley's, she also points out there has been very little research on prostitution and that a sampling of prostitutes across the economic scale would better represent their feelings on the matter. Carol also feels that pointing out a simple disdain for work can skew the weight of results.

"You can't obtain accurate data about the qualities of 'prostitutes in general,' because prostitution is underground," she argues. "Most statistics are obtained from those who are easily accessible to researchers, in the criminal justice system, those who use services at various agencies. The samples are necessarily skewed, but many misrepresent the results to represent prostitution in general."

"Melissa's work tries to prove that prostitutes want to quit, and I think that's sort of an inflammatory way to view prostitution," she explains. "Of course they want to quit; most people want to change jobs to a job that's more secure, that has benefits. I agree with her there, but I just wouldn't necessarily frame it as oppression."

In Carol's opinion, the solution lies not in stricter sentences for johns, but legalization of prostitution and more rights for the sex worker.

"The way [prostitution] is practiced in our society is often oppressive," she says, "and criminalization makes it more oppressive."

In fact, says Carol, it is work like Farley's which enforces the polarization of views on prostitution, by enforcing the stereotype that there are two kinds of prostitutes: the "happy hooker," as Farley says, and the quintessential victim—the oppressed, miserable, drug-addicted prostitute.

"Matters of choice and sex are a continuum," she explains. "Not just polar opposites."

However, Carol concedes that Farley's research accurately represents *some* prostitutes—what percentage of the world's prostitutes that is, she doesn't know.

"I understand that Melissa's research does not necessarily represent the 'happy hooker,'" she explains. "I just think the fundamentalist feminist agenda creates only a narrow framework for 'appropriate sex.' People have sex for a lot of different reasons."

Access to Escape

While COYOTE and Danzine argue that unionizing will unite prostitutes under labor laws, Nikki, Swana, and Farley object to organizations like Danzine and COYOTE, because they believe that, legal or not, prostitution will always reflect the racial and class status.

"The thing I would say is most typical of groups which advocate prostitution is that they are composed largely of white European Americans," explains Farley. "These women are not poor or working class. In other words, these are women who have access to escapes from prostitution, who decide they want $4000 to pay tuition for a semester."

LOTUS sees Danzine as a threat, because it gives people an excuse to look at prostitution as a viable form of income. People don't have to feel guilty about going to strip clubs, watching porn, etc.

"It's not a pretty sight to see an older prostituted woman," says Nikki. "That's why I think pro-prostitution groups get so much more attention. No one wants to see the reality of a 40-year-old prostituted woman who looks 90. It's more pleasing to look at a perky 18-year-old who seems healthy."

The by-product of this ignorance, argues Nikki, is a systematic ignorance and system of oppression within prostitution. The consequences for a woman caught in prostitution are significantly higher than those for a john; in 1993, 42 percent of women arrested in Seattle on prostitution-related charges were convicted. In the same year, eight percent of men arrested in Seattle on prostitution-related charges were convicted.

Moreover, in Oregon, when a woman is convicted of prostitution, she's convicted of a sex crime—the same category in which child molesters fall. Because of the severity of that category, children are more easily taken away from these women, and they can never qualify for federal housing or have a job working with kids. In Portland, Nikki watches johns who have been arrested regularly walk away with $25 fines, while the prostitutes they were working with are charged with sex crimes.

While COYOTE and Danzine agree that oppression within prostitution exists, by legalizing prostitution, argues Carol, the government will legally owe women certain guarantees of safety and privilege, regardless of class status. Moreover, the power would lie in the hands of prostitutes and sex workers themselves—rather than pimps and social workers.

Nevertheless, the heart of the disagreement between the two groups comes down to one issue: whether prostitution is a choice or a form of oppression.

For Nikki, the answer is clear. "After doing outreach in jail, the women say to me, 'Nikki, I never looked at prostitution like that. I thought it was my choice.'"

CONTEMPORARY
ISSUES
COMPANION

CHAPTER 2

Is Prostitution a Serious Problem?

Prostitution Is an Evil Institution

Dorn Checkley

Dorn Checkley is the director of WholeHearted, an organization that promotes biblical sexual values. In the following article, Checkley discusses Alexa Albert's Brothel: Mustang Ranch and Its Women, *a book about legal prostitution in Nevada brothels. Checkley contends that Albert glosses over or ignores the problems inherent in legalized prostitution, such as boyfriends who act as pimps and take all the prostitutes' earnings, the exploitation of prostitutes, and a continuing black market for prostitution. Checkley maintains that prostitution is wrong because intimacy—which is a big part of sex—cannot be bought. Furthermore, he asserts that prostitution undermines marriage. Checkley concludes that prostitution is an evil institution that should not be legalized.*

Early one morning on June 6th [2003] I caught the opening salvos to a new battle in the old war for sexual values while I was watching NBC's *The Today Show*. Host Matt Lauer interviewed Dr. Alexa Albert, the author of a . . . nonfiction book entitled, *Brothel: Mustang Ranch and Its Women*. The author is a medical doctor who was allowed to study the former Mustang Ranch brothel in Nevada to find out why its incidents of sexually transmitted diseases [STDs] were so low. She published that study, but separately researched and wrote this book about the lifestyles of the prostitutes and their customers. The interview featured most of the clichés that we have all come to expect in the war for sexual values. If you are familiar with those clichés you could have written the book yourself.

Dorn Checkley, "Legalized Prostitution? Beware the New Campaign to Solve an Old Problem," WholeHearted, August 5, 2003. Reproduced by permission.

A "Touching" Story

Responding to Matt Lauer's "probing" questions, Dr. Albert recounted that she entered the study with the preconceived idea that prostitution was "a dehumanizing, objectifying business that did women real damage." Of course, once she got to know the prostitutes she realized that these are actually hardworking women who support children, sick parents or were working their way through medical school—blah, blah, blah. She told a "touching" story of a father who brought his son to be sexually initiated by one of the women. The teenager had a confidence-destroying experience with her due to performance anxiety and inexperience. The doctor said the woman blamed herself and felt very guilty. Matt knowingly smiled. Dr. Albert smiled back. Ah, the prostitute with a heart of gold.

Great cliché. Testosterone laden-control freak dad meets heart-for-gold prostitute and produces sexually dysfunctional teen who will grow up to be: a) an internet porn addict who avoids sex with his wife because he can't maintain an erection; b) a guilt-ridden homosexual in search of a father figure or; c) a serial killer of prostitutes whose crime spree gets featured in 2015's TV movie event of the year. Way to go.

Dr. Albert went on to describe a clean, disease-free workplace where the prostitutes are relatively safe from violence, exploitation and drugs. She also came to appreciate the sexual predilections of the customers or "johns." When Matt asked her what she thought about the "johns" she said she was surprised by the "diversity" of the clients and their sexual "needs."

I'm sure that you get the script by now. Dr. Albert asserted that this exploitive, dehumanizing sexual practice is not really that way at all if we would just get over our old fashioned notions. If we would just see these prostitutes as hard working women and their "johns" as men with "unmet sexual needs," then we could all move forward to a more diverse culture that no longer stigmatizes "the world's oldest profession."

You can be absolutely sure that you will see Dr. Albert making the rounds of all the talk shows in the near future to promote her book. And the script will remain the same.

Asking Different Questions

I wish that I could get a shot at her. I would love to ask some of the questions Matt failed to ask.

Dorn: Well, Dr. Albert, I started my career as a counselor to runaway and homeless youth in Times Square, New York City. A few years later you did the same for a summer internship. In my experience the prostitute who comes from a stable two-parent home and is working her way through college is by far the exception to the rule—an exaggeration of the media and not the real picture. Over a three-year period I counseled a couple of dozen prostitutes and erotic dancers and nearly all of them claimed they liked what they were doing. Of course, they were just rationalizing. And surviving. We knew that these young girls were kicked out of their homes or were physically or sexually abused. They dropped out of high school and had virtually no marketable skills. Our job wasn't to pat them on the back and say, "you go girl!" Our job was to love and challenge them—to expand their life options, not limit them. In the end your book ratifies the lifestyle of legalized prostitution. Are you sure that you are seeing things for what they really are?

Dorn: Dr. Albert, your book advocates legalizing prostitution in brothels, as opposed to "street walking," for the safety of the women and the low rate of STDs. However, your book details that many problems surrounding prostitution still exist in brothels. For example, you spent an entire chapter exposing the fact that the majority of the women you met still had "pimps"! Many of the women call them "boyfriends," but they still give these men large sums of their money. You reported that the police have busted a prostitution ring from Oregon that placed their women in the Nevada brothels. There was even a case where a girl's mother "turned her out," as they say, just to support her. Finally, you report that the brothels knowingly support pimps because "a girl with a pimp works harder." *With all this evidence from your own book*, how can you assert that women will not be exploited in future brothels across the country when they are presently exploited in Nevada's legal brothels?

Dorn: Dr. Albert, your book is now an argument for a significant change in public policy, namely to legalize prostitution like they have done in the Netherlands. However, an investigation of international prostitution by journalist Christine Dolan for the International Center for Missing & Exploited Children found that illegal prostitution is flourishing in the Netherlands and other parts of Europe. Third-world women are being kidnapped and sold into sexual slavery in European brothels. Although it is illegal, young teens and even children are being prostituted in the Netherlands, and child pornography is flourishing there as well. Are you sure that we should get on this slippery slope? Despite all the best intentions, the proof is coming in that the Netherlands haven't been able to stop the black market for prostitutes; haven't stopped international pimps from exploiting vulnerable women; *and* they have become a defacto international safety zone for the trade of child pornography. Do we really want all that? Is it really possible to clean up this dirty business?

Oh well, fantasies work better than real life. I'm sure that Dr. Albert would have perfectly plausible answers to my sharp questions. And why shouldn't she? In a culture that exalts "diversity" and self-styled morality above all else, all answers are equal.

Why Prostitution Is Wrong

So why do we at "WholeHearted" think that prostitution is still wrong?

It is wrong first because even mere sex, like love, can never be truly bought. Sexual pleasure is either mutually given in a state of marital love, or it is a cheap imitation of the real thing. Of course the proponents of prostitution argue that johns and prostitutes are not so naive, but here again Dr. Albert's own book undermines her case. She spends two chapters detailing anecdotes about johns becoming emotionally attached to the women they buy and seeking romance that inevitably fails. These men swagger into the brothel with a cavalier attitude and a calloused heart to buy a good time, but find the very act of sex engenders emotional attachments they did not anticipate. Other men are tragic lonely hearts seeking to buy the intimacy and love that they have been unable to find in real life. They are destined to never be truly satisfied. Why should society allow sex—an act intrinsic to human love, dignity and family—to become a mere commodity?

Prostitution is wrong secondly because it undermines marriage. Dr. Albert's book fails to examine this consequence at all. Sexual disease is a problem. Forced exploitation is a problem. However, in Dr. Albert's moral universe the consequences to marriage and family don't seem to exist. Legalized prostitution will proliferate and gain legitimacy, just like pornography has, but legal and social acceptance will never ameliorate the negative consequences to marriage. Libertines can talk a good game, but no one really likes to be cheated on and no one really likes sexual competition. It will always hurt at a deep level. And the consequences of broken marriages have profound ramifications to society. We don't need any more negative pressure on marriage in our culture.

Prostitution is wrong finally because women, men, and sex are degraded by it. No matter what law is passed or propaganda campaign undertaken, prostitutes will always be exploited second-class women. Don't believe the utopian dreams of the sexual revolutionists. Believe thousands of years of 'the world's oldest profession' and the nature of humankind. We are not going to change our natures. Men and sex are just as degraded. When sex is divorced from love and marriage, and bartered like a commodity, men will descend to savagery. Or at least to the Peter Pan–syndromed, marriage allergic, porn-addicted facsimile that passes for millions of men today. We desperately need to elevate the value and dignity of sex right now and not lower it any more.

A Lack of a Moral Framework

Why doesn't Dr. Albert 'get it'? Dr. Albert's key deficiency in analyzing brothel prostitution is that her compassion lacks a moral framework. Underneath the bizarre lifestyle and the attendant evils of the business, she found the prostitutes' humanity. That's very good. Jesus did too. When he allowed the "sinful woman" to wash his feet; when he "saved" the woman caught in adultery from unjust stoning; when he consorted with tax gatherers and prostitutes—Jesus saw past their sin and found their humanity. *But he went further than Dr. Albert seems capable of doing. He also told them to "go and sin no more."*

Jesus fully embodied a characteristic that does not come easily to us mere humans: He was compassionate and just at the same time. He understood prostitutes; He demonstrated compassion towards prostitutes; but He did not excuse their behavior. Some Christians are full of condemnation for the sin but show no compassion for the sinner. The Godly way is to demonstrate both. It is one of the deepest manifestations of love.

Prostitution as an institution is evil. It doesn't matter if it is the "world's oldest profession," it is still wrong. However, prostitutes themselves are not evil and neither are their johns. They are usually broken and needy individuals seemingly trapped by the circumstances of their lives. Ultimately, to accept and legitimize prostitutes and johns is not compassionate; it is lazy. Not to undertake the difficult task of leading, encouraging and calling them to the higher way is a failure to love as Jesus would have loved them.

Legalized Prostitution Contributes to Sex Trafficking

Dorchen A. Leidholdt

Dorchen A. Leidholdt is the co–executive director of the Coalition Against Trafficking in Women. The following selection is an excerpt of a speech she gave about sex trafficking in which she maintains that legalized prostitution contributes to sex trafficking. She states that some countries, such as Germany, opened legalized brothels in hopes of stemming street prostitution and its spread of sexually transmitted diseases. However, these small brothels could not fulfill the demand of numerous sex tourists. Leidholdt says that partial legalization simply suggested that these governments were supportive of prostitution, and sex crimes and illegal prostitution flourished. This encouraged the abduction and trafficking in women, usually undocumented immigrants, in these countries. Leidholdt concludes that trafficking cannot be differentiated from prostitution; they are one and the same, and both are tragic phenomena that should be ended.

I flew into Frankfurt [Germany] on my way to Strasbourg [France], and used that opportunity to study, up close, legalized prostitution, European-style. The Frankfurt city fathers had created a system of legal, regulated brothels, hoping to stamp out an array of evils, including street prostitution, control of the sex industry by organized crime, and the spread of sexually transmitted diseases. It was obvious that their strategy was a colossal failure. Street prostitution was flourishing; organized crime groups were running underground brothels filled with Asian, Latin American, and Eastern European women and girls. Only the few legal brothels (grossly outnumbered by their underground counterparts) cared whether buyers used condoms.

Dorchen A. Leidholdt, "Demand and the Debate," http://action.web.ca/home/catw/attach/leidholdtspeechOct03.com, October 2003. Reproduced by permission of the author.

A Two-Tiered System

What had emerged in Frankfurt was a two-tiered system of prostitution. I later realized that this was the face of legalized prostitution in the western world. Women and girls who had been trafficked from poor countries were propelled into a competition with Western-born women for local prostitution customers and a growing number of sex tourists. It was apparent that the quotient of suffering was the most acute for the undocumented women and girls in the illegal brothels. They were forced to endure unwanted sex with half-a-dozen customers each night, were unable to protect themselves from HIV and other sexually transmitted diseases, and were deprived of travel documents, threatened with violence and deportation, and required to work off exorbitant debt that locked them into conditions of slavery.

While not as dire as that of their internationally trafficked sisters, the lot of the legally prostituted women was also dismal. Posing as an American newspaper reporter, I was welcomed by the madam into a legal brothel in the heart of Frankfurt. It resembled a four-star hotel in the United States. I was soon surrounded by a group of women eager for a distraction from their late afternoon wait for their "clients." Several of the women's husbands were also their pimps, most of the women were from poor, rural areas of Germany, and all faced bleak futures with few employment skills. The sex of prostitution was an unwanted invasion they had developed a series of strategies to avoid—their favorite, they confided, was to get the men so drunk that they didn't know what they were penetrating. The women seemed bored and depressed. Their depression deepened when I asked them what they hoped to be doing in five years. Aside from one woman who said that she hoped to help manage the brothel, they were at a loss for words.

The effects of trafficking and prostitution were not confined to the brothels in Frankfurt. I was told by Asian women working to assist trafficking victims that they couldn't publish their names in the telephone books or they got calls all night long from prostitution buyers. They were constantly solicited for sex. The mainstream media was saturated with prostitution imagery.

When I boarded the train to Strasbourg, it seemed indisputable to me that prostitution and sex trafficking were interrelated phenomena. . . .

Globalized Prostitution

What is the relation if any between prostitution and sex trafficking? The truth is that what we call sex trafficking is nothing more or less than globalized prostitution. Sex industry profiteers transport girls and women across national and regional borders and "turn them out" into prostitution in locations in which their victims are least able to resist and where there is the greatest demand for them. Ironically, the demand is greatest in countries with organized women's movements, where the status of women is high and there are relatively few local women available for commercial sexual exploitation. The brothels of the United States, Canada, the Netherlands, Germany, Austria, and Australia are filled with women trafficked from Asia, Latin America, and Eastern Europe. No less than 50% of German prostitutes are illegal immigrants and a staggering 80% of Dutch prostitutes are not Dutch-born.

Conversely, what most people refer to as "prostitution" is usually domestic trafficking. The bulk of the sex industry involves pimps and other sex industry entrepreneurs controlling women and girls, often by moving them from places in which they have family and friends into locations in which they have no systems of support. Movement is also essential because customers demand novelty. In the United States, for example, there are national and regional sex industry circuits in which prostituted women and girls are rotated among cities, ensuring customers variety and sex industry entrepreneurs control.

Overlapping Characteristics of Trafficking and Prostitution

Sex trafficking and prostitution overlap in fundamental ways. Those targeted for commercial sexual exploitation share key characteristics: poverty, youth, minority status in the country of exploitation, histories of abuse, and little family support. Sex industry customers exploit trafficked and prostituted women interchangeably, for the identical purpose. The sex industry businesses in which trafficked and prostituted women are exploited are often one and the same, with trafficked and locally prostituted women "working" side by side. Local brothels and strip clubs are usually traffickers' destinations and key to their financial success. The injuries that prostituted and trafficked women suffer are identical: post-traumatic stress disorder, severe depression, damage to reproductive systems, damage from sexual assault and beatings, and sexually transmitted diseases.

Certainly international trafficking intensifies the dynamics of power and control that characterize domestic prostitution: the isolation of the victims; their dependence on their abusers; their difficulty in accessing criminal justice and social service systems; and their fear of exposure to the authorities. But the dynamics of trafficking and prostitution are the same dynamics, and their commonalities far overshadow their differences. In spite of efforts to differentiate and separate prostitution and trafficking, the inescapable conclusion is that the difference between the two, at most, is one of degree, not of kind.

Opposing Policies

If sex trafficking and prostitution were distinct and separate phenomena, and if prostitution were as innocuous as trafficking is injurious, a logical response would be to direct criminal sanctions against sex traffickers and legalize and regulate prostitution. This is the position that the Netherlands, Germany, and others following the "Dutch" example have embraced. But the Dutch and German experience—along with those of other jurisdictions that have legalized prostitution—have demonstrated just what happens when prostitution is legitimized and protected by law: the number of sex businesses grows, as does the demand for prostitution. Legalized prostitution brings sex tourists and heightens the demand among local men. Local women constitute an inadequate supply so foreign girls and women are trafficked in to meet the demand. The trafficked women are cheaper, younger, more exciting to customers, and easier to control. More trafficked women means more local demand and more sex tourism. The end result looks a lot like Amsterdam [in the Netherlands].

The Swedish government, in response to the massive movement of trafficked Eastern European women into its borders, developed an antithetical policy response. In 1999, it passed and implemented legislation that stepped up measures against prostitution not only by directing strong penalties against pimps, brothel owners, and other sex industry entrepreneurs but by also directing criminal sanctions against customers. (The law also eliminated penalties against prostitutes, such as the penalty for soliciting.) After the passage of the new law, Sweden spearheaded a public education campaign warning sex industry customers that patronizing prostitutes was criminal behavior. The result was unexpected. While there was not a dramatic decrease in the incidence of prostitution, sex trafficking to Sweden declined while neighboring Scandanavian countries witnessed a significant increase. The danger of prosecution coupled with a diminished demand made Sweden an unpromising market for global sex traffickers.

The antithetical Dutch and Swedish legislative approaches to prostitution and trafficking hold important lessons for social change activists and policy makers. Legalizing and legitimizing domestic prostitution throws out a welcome mat to international sex traffickers. Curtailing the demand for prostitution chills sex trafficking.

A Human Rights Catastrophe

Prostitution and sex trafficking are the same human rights catastrophe, whether in local or global guise. Both are part of a system of gender-based domination that makes violence against women and girls profitable to a mind-boggling extreme. Both prey on women and girls made vulnerable by poverty, discrimination, and violence and leaves them traumatized, sick, and impoverished. Both reward predators sexually and financially, strengthening both the demand and criminal operations that ensure the supply. The concerted effort by some NGO's [nongovernmental organizations] and governments to disconnect trafficking from prostitution—to treat them as distinct and unrelated phenomena—is nothing less than a deliberate political strategy aimed at legitimizing the sex industry and protecting its growth and profitability.

The obvious fact that the demand for prostitution and the demand for trafficked women are one [and] the same demonstrates the fallacy of this false division. It also reveals our best hope for ending trafficking and prostitution. . . . As the Swedish government has shown in arresting buyers, while demand is essential to sex industry success it also represents the weak link in the sex industry chain. Unlike prostituted women and girls, prostitution customers do have choices to make. And when they see that choosing to buy women devastates lives and threatens their own freedom and social standing, they make different choices. We've seen what works. The domestic violence movement has witnessed a dramatic decline in repeat domestic violence and the incidence of intimate partner homicides following a decades-long program of education, support and services for victims, and, crucially, accountability for abusers through a pro-arrest, pro-prosecution approach. Curtailing the demand for prostitution through accountability for prostitution buyers is the essential next step in our fight to end trafficking and prostitution.

Child Prostitution Is a Serious Problem

Bay Fang

In the following article Bay Fang describes how thousands of teenage girls are tricked every year into becoming prostitutes by their "boyfriends" who are actually pimps. The younger the girl is, the more in demand she is, Fang says, and the higher the price she can charge her customers. Yet despite the large amounts of money that girl prostitutes make each night, they rarely get to keep any of it; it is all handed over to their pimps. Even though many girls periodically seek safety in social service shelters, Fang states, few remain for long. Most return to the streets and prostitution. Fang is a correspondent for U.S. News & World Report.

Kristie was 13 when she met the first of her four "daddies." She had run away from home in the Southwest, and friends introduced her to a tall, good-looking man, who said the red-haired teenager was sexy and had potential. Pretty soon, he had her prostituting herself on the streets of Las Vegas—and then Los Angeles, Atlanta, and Phoenix. She and her "wifies," the other girls working under the same pimp, most of whom were also in their teens, would be brought to a city, work from 7 p.m. until sunrise, then move on. The now 15-year-old (who, like the other girls, doesn't want her real name used) stopped only after she was arrested, in July [2005]. From the beginning of the year until then, she estimates, she had over 100 sex partners—but she had long since stopped counting.

The trafficking in children for sex was once thought to be a problem beyond America's borders. But the FBI and the Justice Department have now started focusing intently on the issue—and what they've found is shocking. Thousands of young girls and boys are falling victim to violent pimps, who move them from state to state, which makes it a federal matter. The younger they are, the more they're worth on the street. "There is a greater and greater demand for younger and younger kids," says Ernie Allen, president of the National Center for Missing and Exploited Children [NCMEC]. "America doesn't look. People are shocked and horrified when they hear these girls' stories. They say, 'That doesn't happen here. It happens in Thailand. Or the Philippines.' But once you start shining a light on it, you find it everywhere."

Getting Serious

[In 2003], the FBI and the Justice Department launched something called the Innocence Lost initiative. More than 40 FBI agents have been dedicated to task forces in the 14 cities with the highest incidence of child prostitution—places like Atlanta, Detroit, and Minneapolis. Since the campaign's inception, the feds have obtained almost 40 federal indictments of accused sex traffickers and pimps. [In October 2005], a federal grand jury indicted Jaron Brice, 29—also known as "Jay Bird" and "Daddy" —in Washington, D.C., on 17 counts related to the sex trafficking of minors. And "in a few months," says David Johnson, director of the Crimes Against Children unit of the FBI, "there will be a round of cases that is bigger than anything that's happened before. We are not looking just to do a quick arrest; we are trying to remove an entire enterprise."

The roots of Innocence Lost can be found in investigations begun in Oklahoma City back in 2003, after a series of murders of prostitutes who worked at truck stops. "We went out and said, 'Is there some federal intervention we could do to combat all this violent crime?'" says Mike Beaver, the FBI Crimes Against Children coordinator in Oklahoma City. "The more we looked, the more we determined that we needed to work child prostitution." The investigations led to the discovery of a loose network of more than 45 pimps and over 100 prostitutes, who recruited girls from Oklahoma City and followed trucking routes to Denver, Miami, Houston, and Dallas. Fourteen pimps have since been convicted on federal charges as a result of the Oklahoma City probes, with sentences as long as 210 months. Three major interstates cross Oklahoma City, and the truck stops here, such as Pilot and TravelCenters of America, are like little cities, with everything from restaurants to TV lounges. The parking lots can cover acres. The back row of each lot is known as "Party Row," and the truckers know that's where the girls are. Law enforcement officers monitoring CB radio traffic regularly hear girls ask, "Hey truckers, anyone want some commercial company?" If someone responds, they switch to a different frequency, then get down to business. "I'm blond-haired, blue-eyed, 34C . . . if you want to play with this baby doll, tell me what color your house is," she will say, referring to his truck. He will often flash his lights so she knows where to go. A girl can have dozens of "dates" a night but will not stop until she has made her "trap," the amount of money she has to bring home to her pimp.

Ownership

Cindy (not her real name) is 14, with dyed blond hair and an $800 trap. Her pimp was Michael Thomas, FBI officials say, whose street name was "1–8," a reference to time in an Oklahoma City gang. He had tattooed on his girls' bodies the letters POE, for "Pimpin' One Eight." He would buy girls from other pimps, for as little as $50, give them names like Orgasm, and send them out to truck stops, charging $60 for oral sex, $80 for intercourse, and $100 for both. When Cindy told Thomas she wanted to leave his "stable," he had another girl stab her in her arms and hands, according to the FBI.

A University of Pennsylvania study from 2001 estimates that close to 300,000 children nationwide are at risk of falling victim to some sort of sexual exploitation. Outreach workers concur, saying that of the 1 million to 1.5 million runaway children in the country, about a third have some brush with prostitution. "When we began initiating investigations around the country," says Johnson, "we found it everywhere we looked."

On the "strolls" of Sunset Boulevard and Figueroa, in South-Central Los Angeles, girls step out from the shadows in tiny skirts and stiletto heels. Detective Keith Haight sizes them up. He doesn't bother stopping unless they look underage, but it's hard to tell nowadays. Haight has been working these streets for 25 years and has seen the girls getting younger. This drop in age is due both to the rise of the Internet, which provides ready access to child pornography, and to the fear of HIV/AIDS. "Back then, if you found a 15- or 16-year-old, that was a big deal. But now, they're 11 or 12," he says. "If you go to the bus station, you can see the runaways coming off the buses, and you can tell the pimps waiting for them."

Many of today's pimps have gang ties, and they've moved from murder and robbery to pimping. "There has been a trend of organized crime moving away from traditional commodities like drugs, tobacco, and arms, to kids," says NCMEC's Allen. "They are reusable, inexpensive, with a huge consumer market that is enormously profitable with next to no risk. Nobody cares. Nobody is looking for them. They are the forgotten."

Kristie has a ponytail and eyes that dart around the room. Sometimes, it's easy to forget that the articulate teenager prowling for johns is just that—a teenage girl. She glibly instructs a visitor on how to outsmart the vice cops. "You never offer anything until you're up in the room with him," she says. "You tell them you're a private dancer. When you hug him, make sure he only has one wallet—if he has another lump, it could be a badge. Check to see that there's luggage in his room, with the tags still on it. And always, always, say you're 18."

Eyes and Smiles

At truck stops in California, girls often wear jeans and carry a backpack, looking as if they're studying. "But there is something about their eyes, and the way they smile at you, that tells you they're not just regular kids," says James Morrow, an outreach worker for a nonprofit called Children of the Night, who used to frequent truck stops to educate both the girls and the truckers—until threats from the pimps made that too dangerous. Sometimes the same girls will travel to Texas, Arizona, and Oklahoma, greeting truckers in each place by name.

The girls' stories sound scarily similar. Kristie's parents are divorced, and she was raped at the age of 8 by one of her mother's boyfriends. Linda, a 14-year-old from Arizona, never met her father. She was raped repeatedly by her stepbrothers when she was 6 and 7, and she fell in with a pimp who convinced her to start prostituting herself when she was 13.

Because of their backgrounds, many of the girls just crave attention. "I wanted someone to look out for me," says Fay, who grew up in a wealthy family in New York City but was left by her parents to be brought up by strict grandparents. "I needed a father—someone older, who could figure out my little tricks." Pimps play mind games to make their prostitutes compete with one another for attention. "I felt wanted all the time—by somebody," explains Kristie. "I felt like I was good at something."

"Baptized"

Pimps also use the promise of riches to entice girls into "the Game." But while the girls can make thousands of dollars a night, they never keep much of it. If they do, they get "baptized," or beaten by their pimps. Kristie's pimp would rape her if she did not bring in enough money, saying things like, "I know you don't want Daddy to do it like this, but you have to be punished." "The average life expectancy of a child after getting into prostitution," says Johnson, citing homicide or HIV/AIDS as the main causes of death, "is seven years." Tom O'Brien, the criminal division chief of the Los Angeles U.S. attorney's office, describes a conversation he had with one 14-year-old prostitute who was testifying against her pimp. "I told her, 'When I was your age, I thought I'd live forever.' She looked me in the eye and said, 'Mr. O'Brien, I'll be dead before I'm 21.'"

Children of the Night is housed in a nondescript building in the San Fernando Valley. A big teddy bear on the counter greets visitors, and the dorm-like rooms are plastered with posters of pop stars. The difference between this and a regular boarding school is that the teenagers here are all former prostitutes. They have parole officers, social workers, therapists. They are tested every week for HIV/AIDS. A list in the office keeps track of when and where each girl has to testify against her pimp. When Lois Lee started this program 26 years ago, local government social services agencies told her they couldn't take in prostitutes. She says that the new federal interest is a step in the right direction. "But what do you do with them once you've got them?" she asks. "Where's the love, the family, the programs, the schools?"

Kristie has been at the shelter for three weeks, and she says, with a toss of her head, that she thinks she'll stay. She has been arrested twice, she says, but the first time, she said to her parole officer, "I'm not going to stay here. I know California like the back of my hand. You won't be able to find me." When she was released from juvenile detention hall, she immediately cut off her parole bracelet and ran away, back to the streets. Haight, sitting in his car on Sunset Boulevard, says he has seen hundreds like her—and more coming in every day. "It's like America has lost its innocence," the detective says. "Little girls just aren't little girls anymore."

Male Prostitutes Are Often Overlooked

Vic St. Blaise

The following article is written by Vic St. Blaise, a sex worker activist and a prostitute. He maintains that male prostitutes—while vastly outnumbered by female prostitutes—are overlooked by researchers studying prostitution and by services geared to prostitutes. Legal and political policies designed to help prostitutes or deter prostitution also largely fail to address male prostitutes. St. Blaise contends that one reason male prostitutes are overlooked is perhaps their publicly ambiguous sexual identity. That is, while male prostitutes have sex with men, many do not consider themselves to be homosexual. In addition, he asserts, male prostitutes are almost invisible on the street, compared to the numerous female prostitutes, who tend to wear easily recognizable attire.

Men are as much a part of the sex industry as women, and while we are at it, let's not forget our transgendered co-workers. As the task force member 'representing gay male sex workers,' I offer my observations and theories involved in my participation in the task force, sex work, and the sex workers' rights movement. Men in the sex industry and the rights movement must be prepared to face homophobia and invisibility in addition to the traditional ignorance of and hostility toward the profession.

Women and Children First

Most people, if not all, when they hear the word 'prostitute' automatically assume the feminine gender. This is understandable to a point. I am sure there are many more women in

Vic St. Blaise, "Issues for Male Sex Workers," testimony before the San Francisco Task Force on Prostitution, November 1994. Reproduced by permission of the author.

prostitution than men. If we accept that around 80 to 90 percent of the population is heterosexual, and that in general women seldom use the services of prostitutes, then it stands to conclude that the majority of customers are heterosexual men.

Unfortunately the development of the arguments for or against prostitution and studies on prostitution have until recently continued on a gender bias, with no concern for men involved in prostitution, either as workers, or more glaringly, as clients. Policies, services, research and rhetoric have chosen to participate in the battle between men (clients, cops) vs. women (prostitutes), instead of looking at prostitution as a ubiquitous ingredient of the human experience.

This bias is a by-product of sexism in our society that oppresses women at every turn. Those who are against prostitution see the profession as yet another example of violence against women by men. Prostitution advocates see sex work as a way for women to empower themselves, at the expense, literally, of men. Sex workers of other genders do not fit easily into the equation, and no one has known what to do with us beyond the recognition that we exist.

Another part of the problem of sexism is the assumption that men in the industry do not need protection, rights or support. Since men cause all the problems in prostitution, what do male sex workers have to worry about? Surely a man would not attempt with another man the same sh** he tries with women. Again, the narrow men vs. women model of prostitution ignores the other combinations, but the erroneous assumption that guys can handle themselves is reflected in the amount of services and education geared toward men in the industry.

What precarious support there is exists in the form of rescuing boys, since the rescuing of children shares similar popularity with the rescuing of women. Recently a network called CASH, Coalition Advocating Safer Hustling, grew out of an

AmFAR [American Foundation for AIDS Research] grant set up to study the prevention of HIV/AIDS among male sex workers. The original constitution was amended, in part to accommodate the cries of protest from agencies that felt the organization presented a too strong pro-prostitution message. Because there are so few organizations that work with male sex workers, CASH toned down its press, if not its intent. Although it includes transgender sex workers in its charter, CASH continues to struggle to maintain a healthy number of participants.

Homophobia and Sexphobia

I have encountered what I perceive to be homophobia among members of the task force as well as [among] prostitute advocates, and sexphobia among gay men, in addition to whorephobia from all angles. Because a male prostitute is such a new animal to many people, those of us who are out and have opinions are easy targets for criticisms based on partially processed assumptions about being a man, being a queer, and being a whore.

Personally I take most of it in stride. I have been fortunate. No one becomes understanding of issues of those different from themselves overnight, and most remarks I let pass without audible comment. If I had to point out every gender-biased comment made during the task force meetings, or at COYOTE [an organization advocating more rights for prostitutes] meetings for that matter, I'd have no voice left. Besides, I have found others willing to correct the non-inclusive statements of others for me, and I see that as an encouraging step.

However, homophobia has darker manifestations for men in the industry. The obsession in this society of labeling based on who you have sex with has resulted in many problems for those who do not conform. Just ask any bisexual.

The man who has sex with men for money but is not gay is another creature who, because he doesn't fit in [to] any of the existing structures, gets placed in whatever cage is left over in the What Are You? zoo. Because sexual identity is such a charged absolute, and because [of] the ramifications of not picking the right answer, these men are in a service and support twilight zone.

The gay community doesn't want them, the sex worker community won't touch them. The guys don't want to be labeled homosexual, they're just having sex with other men. Many outreach workers complain that male street workers are an extremely hard to reach population, in part because of the sexual identity issue. In AIDS services this is a crucial crack in the system.

The Invisible Men

Chances are when walking around Polk Street [in San Francisco] you figure you could pick out the hustlers. But is that guy over there a hustler, or a panhandler, or a drug dealer? Is he a combination? Is he just hanging out waiting for some buddies to show up?

Unlike women who work on the street, there is not a highly recognizable uniform for the men. The clothes I wore on Polk were the same ones I wore to my day job and to the task force meetings. Such a nondescript ensemble would do for any of the activities taking place on the street. No mini skirts, no lipstick, no fishnets [stockings]. We could blend in easily, but you say to yourself, "I know one when I see one." Maybe.

Again because of sexism in general and gender bias in particular, men can and must act differently from our female counterparts when on the street. For reasons I don't completely understand, an initial response of indifference, which can be done with little effort (or noise), is more effective than trying to grab the attention (more effort and noise) of the available johns. The latter works for my female friend on Geary [Street], or for the guy down the street selling drugs, but it would scare away my potential johns.

When statistics, one of my least favorite entities, are slung around the prostitution rink, I duck. If statistics of arrests of prostitutes involve men at all, it is usually to show a bias against women. Women are arrested, men are not, or not as much, more proof that prostitution is stacked against women. There is a term for this kind of faulty deduction, but it escapes me.

Unfortunately, the law does not discriminate. The police may, and we'll get to that, but male sex workers are no less susceptible to the law than female [sex workers]. The first state prison sentence under the . . . mandatory HIV testing law went to a man. True, women arrested as prostitutes outnumber men arrested as prostitutes, and I have my theories.

Again, I would bet my next month's salary that women in prostitution outnumber men vastly. Women are more in demand and can make much more money than men can on the street, where most arrests take place. Men can raise their price by becoming an indoor 'escort'. This involves more work to set up, but if I can charge a client $100 in my home, why would I want to be haggled down to $40 or less on the street?

A woman has more incentive to work outdoors. She has a steady supply of potential clients, even if she is not getting a lot of money per client. Compare the size of the strip on Polk to the areas of the Tenderloin, the Mission and Hayes Valley [other areas in San Francisco] and you will see that there is no reason for any comparison between gender[s] in prostitution arrests.

That is not to say that sexism plays no role. In a society where a man can walk about without a shirt, a woman who appears sexually knowledgeable is a beacon. Sadly, to many she is a threat to civilization and must be controlled. Couple this with the homophobia entrenched in law enforcement and it is easier to guess who will be picked off the street first, a sexily attired woman or a homo who might have AIDS.

Mass media echoes the same reluctance to explore the male sex worker. How many films can you name involving female sex workers? How many male? . . .

To harp just a little more, I was disappointed but not surprised by the lack of interest shown toward me by the mainstream media. Here I was, an active working prostitute who was not in jail or hooked on crack, someone who went about his business without causing crime rates to rise in his neighborhood, someone in good health with an optimistic outlook on life, someone who contributed to his community.

Not one interview, not one question. No one wanted to hear what I had to say about anything. To be fair, I did receive lots of support from certain individuals, especially from those on the Legal and Fiscal Impact Committee [of San Francisco's city government]. I actually felt listened to, and that was great. But when I testified before the city supervisors before my appointment to the task force, I did so envisioning how I was going to explain things to my mom when she saw me on television or in the paper. There is a term for this kind of faulty deduction, and it still escapes me.

Prostitutes Are Regularly Victims of Violence

Melissa Farley

The following selection is an excerpt from an article written by Melissa Farley, a clinical and research psychologist who has been addressing prostitution and sex trafficking for more than a decade. Farley writes that sexual and physical violence are everyday experiences for women involved in prostitution. More than half of the women in numerous prostitution studies have been beaten or raped by their pimps or by their customers and have experienced verbal threats. Furthermore, Farley asserts, women in prostitution do not believe that legalizing prostitution will make them any safer.

It is a cruel lie to suggest that decriminalization or legalization will protect anyone in prostitution. There is much evidence that whatever its legal status, prostitution causes great harm to women. The following sections summarize some of the many studies that now document the physical and emotional harm caused by prostitution.

In the past two decades, a number of authors have documented or analyzed the sexual and physical violence that is the normative experience for women in prostitution.

Violence Is the Norm

Sexual violence and physical assault are the norm for women in all types of prostitution. [Tooru] Nemoto, [Don] Operario, [M.] Takenaka, [Mariko] Iwamoto, and [M. N.] Le reported that 62% of Asian women in San Francisco massage parlors had been physically assaulted by customers. These data were

Melissa Farley, "'Bad for the Body, Bad for the Heart': Prostitution Harms Women Even if Legalized or Decriminalized," *Violence Against Women*, vol. 10, October 2004, pp. 1087–1125. Copyright © 2004 by Melissa Farley. Reproduced by permission of Sage Publications, Inc.

from only 50% of the massage parlors in San Francisco. The other 50%—those brothels controlled by pimps/traffickers who refused entrance to the researchers—were probably even more violent toward the women inside. [Janice G.] Raymond, [Jean] D'Cunha, et al. found that 80% of women who had been trafficked or prostituted suffered violence-related injuries in prostitution. Among the women interviewed by [Ruth] Parriot, 85% had been raped in prostitution. In another study, 94% of those in street prostitution had experienced sexual assault and 75% had been raped by one or more johns. In the Netherlands, where prostitution is legal, 60% of prostituted women suffered physical assaults; 70% experienced verbal threats of physical assault; 40% experienced sexual violence; and 40% had been forced into prostitution or sexual abuse by acquaintances. Most young women in prostitution were abused or beaten by johns as well as pimps. [Mimi H.] Silbert and [Ayala M.] Pines reported that 70% of women suffered rape in prostitution, with 65% having been physically assaulted by customers and 66% assaulted by pimps.

Of 854 people in prostitution in nine countries (Canada, Colombia, Germany, Mexico, South Africa, Thailand, Turkey, United States, and Zambia), 71% experienced physical assaults in prostitution, and 62% reported rapes in prostitution. Eighty-nine percent told the researchers that they wanted to leave prostitution but did not have other options for economic survival. To normalize prostitution as a reasonable job choice for poor women makes invisible their strong desire to escape prostitution.

[Ine] Vanwesenbeeck found that two factors were associated with greater violence in prostitution. The greater the poverty, the greater the violence; and the longer one is in prostitution, the more likely one is to experience violence. Similarly, the more time women spent in prostitution, the more STDs [sexually transmitted diseases] they reported.

Class, Race, and Ethnicity

Those promoting prostitution rarely address class, race, and ethnicity as factors that make women even more vulnerable to health risks in prostitution. [Melissa] Farley found that in NZ [New Zealand] as elsewhere, indigenous women are placed at the bottom of a brutal race and class hierarchy within prostitution itself. When the researchers compared Maori/Pacific Islander New Zealanders to European-origin New Zealanders in prostitution, the Pacific Islander/Maori were more likely to have been homeless and to have entered prostitution at a young age. Mama Tere, an Auckland community activist, referred to NZ prostitution as an "apartheid system." [Libby] Plumridge and [Gillian] Abel similarly described the NZ sex industry as "segmented," noting that 7% of the population in Christchurch were Maori; however, 19% of those in Christchurch prostitution were Maori.

Women in prostitution are treated as if their rapes do not matter. For example, in Venezuela, El Salvador, and Paraguay, the penalty for rape is reduced by one fifth if the victim is a prostitute. Many people assume that when a prostituted woman is raped, that rape is part of her job and that she deserved or even asked for the rape. In an example of this bias, a California judge overturned a jury's decision to charge a customer with rape, saying "a woman who goes out on the street and makes a whore out of herself opens herself up to anybody."

We asked women currently in prostitution in Colombia, Germany, Mexico, South Africa, and Zambia whether they thought that legal prostitution would offer them safety from physical and sexual assault. Forty-six percent of these women in prostitution from six countries felt that they were no safer from physical and sexual assault even if prostitution were legal. Brothel prostitution is legal in Germany, one of the countries surveyed. In an indictment of legal prostitution, 59% of German respondents told us that they did not think that legal prostitution made them any safer from rape and physical assault. A comparable 50% of 100 prostitutes in a Washington, D.C., survey expressed the same opinion.

It is not possible to protect the health of someone whose "job" means that they will get raped on average once a week. One woman explained that prostitution is "like domestic violence taken to the extreme." Another woman said, "What is rape for others, is normal for us."

Arguments Against Prostitution Are Socially Constructed Myths

Cherry Lee

Cherry Lee is the pseudonym of a college professor who did graduate work in human sexuality. In the following selection Lee discusses many of the myths associated with the evils of prostitution. She contends that prohibitions against prostitution stem from ancient times when sexual exclusivity was codified into law to protect a man's "property," in this case, his wife, from other men. She also asserts that the arguments used against prostitution—such as, prostitution harms society or families—have been maintained solely because the perceptions have become embedded in society's traditional beliefs, not because there is any truth to the arguments. She concludes that prostitution is illegal only because society chooses to make it illegal, not because there is any moral reason to make it so.

Sometimes we want to believe things that simply can't be supported by research or facts. One of these areas is *prostitution.*

It is often assumed that most prostitutes are drug addicts and mentally inadequate women that have been forced into a lifestyle that they don't like, but can't escape.

In actual fact, studies have shown that in terms of psychological attributes, prostitutes do not appreciably differ from other women. And, except for "street walkers" controlled by pimps, most appear to have freely chosen to both be in and to stay in the lifestyle.

[Freelance writer] Moira Griffin, writing in an American Bar Association publication, asks, "Are wives and hookers re-

Cherry Lee, "Common Myths About Prostitution," www.moderndirections.com. Reproduced by permission.

ally all that different? Why is a woman who trades sex for money branded a criminal, while a woman who trades sex for domestic services or financial support is accorded society's approbation?"

One answer is that one is seen as providing sex to only one man, and the other to multiple men. . . . Sexual exclusivity was codified into Jewish religious law, and then into civic law, primarily to protect the church and men's *property*. Included in the latter was a man's wife. Later, Jewish law, which by that time had become "God's law," was absorbed into Christian teachings.

With the advent of effective birth control some 50 years ago, and apart from traditional beliefs and the "woman as male property" concept, the original justification for sexual exclusivity has all but disappeared. Even the argument of controlling sexually-transmitted disease [STD], which is still a significant concern, applies less to prostitutes than to the general population. Data suggests that only a small percent of STDs are transmitted by prostitutes, and most of this is by street walkers, many of whom are associated with drugs.

What we might call "the higher-class prostitutes" are even more careful about avoiding STD than the average "girl next door." One of the reasons is that sex is their business, and STD can end their livelihoods—and possibly their lives.

With the male-centered laws against prostitution, men are assuming jurisdiction over how females are allowed to conduct their sexual lives, even though hundreds of thousands of those same men regularly help define the sexual lives of women by using the services of prostitutes.

The Harm-to-Society Argument

Civil Court Judge Margaret Taylor, in handing down a 1978 opinion related to prostitution, said, "The arguments that prostitution harms the public health, safety or welfare do not withstand constitutional scrutiny." A subsequent court, motivated largely by public opinion, felt that Judge Taylor's decision should not be left unchallenged, and succeeded in overturning it.

While it is true that prostitution is often associated with crime, this is due in large measure to the fact that society has pushed it into the unsavory world of criminal activity. After reviewing crime research, Moira Griffin notes, "Many social scientists have concluded that such crime is a byproduct of the environment [to] which society consigns prostitution, rather than being caused by prostitution."

To a significant extent, prostitution is associated with criminality simply because society chooses to define it as a criminal activity.

The Organized Crime Argument

It is widely assumed that organized crime relies on prostitution for a major part of its revenue. This is another myth. Today, only a very small part the money brought in by organized crime activities is related to prostitution. Data suggests that organized crime has turned its efforts to much more profitable white-collar ventures, such as politics, investment, and securities.

The Harm-to-Families Argument

Rather than harm families, an argument can be made that prostitution actually protects the family structure.

First, given the male propensity to seek out new sexual experiences, visiting prostitutes is less threatening to the family unit that seeking out liaisons with single women looking for a husband—or married women dissatisfied with their marriages. The same could be said for women who seek the temporary companionship of "escorts." In both cases the "sex-for-hire" individuals are typically not interested in marriage, or in breaking up a marriage.

Several countries that have legalized prostitution have found no adverse effect on marriages. According to Griffin,

"Prostitution has been practiced for centuries, and disruption of the family has never been causally related to it."

The STD Argument

The issue of prostitution and sexually-transmitted disease (STD) is also a common argument against prostitution. But, as we've noted, only a very small percentage of STD cases can be traced back to prostitutes. Again, the exception is street walkers, who are sometimes associated with drug use.

The "It Destroys the Neighborhood" Argument

The final argument against prostitution is that when the sex trade moves into a neighborhood, prostitutes and their johns become a nuisance and ordinary citizens are harassed. While this is true with some street walkers in some neighborhoods, there are nuisance and harassment laws that clearly cover this. They just have to be enforced.

The sight of prostitutes in a neighborhood and what they represent—"the sin of wanton non-married or extramarital sex"—is what the public typically objects to, which brings us to:

The "Sin" Argument

Organized religion, specifically the Catholic Church, officially feels that sex should be reserved for procreation, and enjoying sex for its own sake is a sin. Interestingly, the Catholic Church condoned prostitution at one point in history, although possibly reluctantly. It was only when the anti-sex movement swept the church hundreds of years after Christianity started that attitudes were reversed. (Biblical scholars feel that Christ, who came from a Jewish background, had a much more open-minded view of sex.)

The sex-is-not-to-enjoy stance is one of the reasons the Catholic Church opposes reliable birth control, despite the fact that it results in three major problems: (1) unwanted children that can't be properly fed, clothed, or educated, (2) friction between a husband and wife, and (3) the husband frequently turning to "other women" for sexual satisfaction.

The general public also has a strange love-hate relationship—or, possibly more accurately, a love-fear relationship—with sex. It tends to feel that sex and love are inextricably associated, even though we know that millions of men and women regularly enjoy sex without being in love.

In addition, millions of affairs take place annually, without a mate knowing; and since the mate does not know, the marriage stays intact.

Since it is well known that sex can be enjoyed without love, one major question is why sex so often supersedes love in dictating whether a marriage stays intact.

The "Having to Provide Sex" Argument

Many people assume that for strictly economic reasons prostitutes have to provide a service that they are basically adverse to. Since many wives find sex is simply a "duty" of marriage, this seems logical.

However, Amy, a former full-time prostitute whom we interviewed, said that she generally enjoyed her work, especially the sex. The fact that she regularly climaxed with the men she spent the night with would seem to support this. After more than two years as a prostitute without contracting an STD or becoming pregnant, Amy found a job with a large U.S. corporation. We should also note that throughout her more than two years as a prostitute, Amy never used drugs or even alcohol. Possibly her case is unusual, but she did report that many of her prostitute friends shared her feelings.

Amy's primary problem with her profession was what people thought about it.

> When I went out with a guy [on a regular date] I always lived in fear that somehow he would find out, and that

would be the end of the relationship.... I never even told [the man I later married] for a long time, until I felt certain he could handle it.... Since I learned to be pretty uninhibited when it comes to sex, [my husband] said that he suspected that I was 'rather experienced,' not that I guess he was complaining, or anything.

... But, I also know that most men couldn't deal with anything like that; so that's a very major problem.... Fortunately, I don't live anywhere near where I worked [as a prostitute], so having one of my old customers recognize me is kind of remote.

The "having to provide sex," anti-prostitution argument is clouded by the fact in many states a wife can't legally claim that she was forced to have sex with her husband against her will. In other words, when it comes to her husband, a rape charge can't be effectively sustained.

Even when regularly abused by a husband, many wives feel that they have no alternative but to stay in the marriage—sometimes with devastating consequences. Each year, more women are killed by husbands than they are by johns or pimps.

This does not mean that prostitution is not a dangerous business. Prostitutes, especially street walkers, are at best considered second-class citizens whose personal welfare isn't valued as much as "decent women." Street walkers frequently get raped, sometimes by policemen who threaten them with imprisonment if they bring charges.

There is no doubt that some women do turn to prostitution to support a drug habit—just as many men turn to crime to support their drug habit. Once this spirals down into the depths of drug dependence, it can represent a slovenly and shameful sight.

The media often focuses on this very real and very tragic element of prostitution. It both supports public perceptions and further encourages politically popular efforts at control.

Interestingly, if the media focused on the six-figure income and jet-set lifestyle of some prostitutes, they know that the public—especially that part of it with young females in the house—would strongly object. It's a message they don't want the media to disseminate, because, however true, it's a message that threatens traditional beliefs. This brings us to:

The Other Side of Prostitution

The negative aspects of prostitution notwithstanding, when you compare the life of a "better class" prostitute with the average woman in the work force, it's easy to see why so many women enter "the life."

Wives and women in the general work force often feel more trapped in their lifestyle than prostitutes [do]. This is due in part because the average female worker earns about 60-cents for every dollar a man makes, and she must often struggle to survive economically.

Plus, no matter how talented they are or how hard they work, it seems that many women in the general work force sooner or later confront the "glass ceiling" that keeps them from moving up to the six-figure executive positions held almost exclusively by men. The income of the "better class" of prostitute can easily exceed six figures. A prostitute can make more in one day than the average waitress or office worker can make in a week.

There are also non-economic reasons for choosing this lifestyle.

Not being anchored to an office, her time is also much more flexible. Since the average prostitute has one child, this gives her time to be with her children. Higher class prostitutes frequently have the opportunity to travel, often with clients who pay the bills.

While it might be argued that a large part of the success of a prostitute depends on her beauty and not all women are endowed with this advantage, we also have to concede that a large part of any person's success depends upon factors such as latent intelligence, or in the case of sports, physical agility—factors that they simply have been "endowed with." . . .

In general in the United States, we are confronting centuries of belief that has embedded itself into the fabric of our thinking. When all the myths are dispelled, what we often come down to with many people is, in effect, "Prostitution should stay illegal because it's obviously wrong." Facts to the contrary are irrelevant.

Unfortunately, if we've learned anything from history, it's that this type of thinking, even as widely accepted as it may have been at the time, has resulted in all manner of human problems and tragedies that could have been avoided.

Prostitution Is Beneficial

Decriminalize Prostitution Now Coalition

Decriminalize Prostitution Now Coalition is dedicated to decriminalizing private, consensual adult prostitution. In the following selection the coalition argues that prostitution actually benefits society by fulfilling the sexual and emotional needs of men and women. By offering their services to men, female prostitutes can teach men intimacy and reduce sexual violence. Furthermore, the coalition states that prostitution can also offer high-paid employment for women and be a satisfying job for them in many ways.

It is long overdue for private, consenting adult prostitution to be decriminalized in the U.S. There are millions of sexworkers in the U.S. who enjoy their profession and the largest risk is not bad clients, not STD's, since most insist on safe sex, but the law enforcement stings wasting resources on morality crimes with no victims.

Prostitution fills a vital role in our society by addressing the sexual and emotional needs of men and women, and by providing high-paying employment options to women and men who wish to provide sexual services.

People in a free society have the right to work in their chosen profession, and to do with their own bodies as they so choose. Likewise, all citizens have the right to engage in consensual adult sexual contact.

Criminalization of private adult prostitution is wrong. Almost all the rest of the world realizes this, and the U.S. is one of the few countries where private sexwork is illegal.

Decriminalize Prostitution Now Coalition, "15 Reasons Why Prostitution Is Beneficial," www.sexwork.com. Reproduced by permission.

Fifteen Reasons Why Prostitution Is Beneficial

1) Sexworkers are a legitimate option for older single men or those married. For example, I gave up the dating game more than 10 years ago. I am just not attracted to most women my age—50s—and was frustrated with "usual" women who are so sexually conservative in our culture. Further, most women in our culture are overweight, to which I have no physical attraction. I find I have far more in common with sexworkers than I do regular women and enjoy younger, slim women—yet with some maturity—so say age 25–35.

For others, they are married but that doesn't always bring sexual satisfaction. Many men enjoy variety and zillions of married men are sexually frustrated since the wife lost interest long ago. Or many of us enjoy intimate sexuality with more than one woman; we enjoy different personalities, bodies, interacting sensually with different women, which also helps us learn good sexual and intimacy skills. Going to sexworkers is far better than an affair and can actually help keep otherwise loving marriages together, if a man gets basic sexual needs met by sexworkers vs. an "affair".

2) Biblically. Not an issue. [Having] many wives and concubines was acceptable, as were "common" prostitutes for Christians; there is clearly nothing wrong for Christians or Jews seeing "common" prostitutes. The only negative references in the Bible is to the sex-goddess prostitutes in the Temples worshiping the fertility gods. It was idolatry—not sex—that was the sin. Many times common prostitutes are mentioned in the Bible with no negative inference. Prostitution has always been legal—for example, in Israel—and Tel Aviv is known as the brothel capital of the world. Yet so many ignorant Christians totally distort biblical sexuality based on negative traditions that have no biblical basis. Likewise, having many wives and concubines was not wrong. A married man never committed adultery as long as the "other woman" was

single—not the property of another man. Adultery was a property sin not a sex sin. For extensive biblical study see... http://www.sexwork.com/coalition/christian.html.

For many Muslims, you marry by reciting certain words. Marriage can be for any length—from 1 minute to 99 years. I have heard of sexworkers with a Muslim client who recites the marriage vows with the time limit, so he feels no guilt since he is married to the sexworker for the time they are having sex. For many Muslims this makes the "arrangement" perfectly legal and is acceptable by the society since you are married! It is called "sigheh." Mohammed, it is said, recommended it to his soldiers and friends. And of course you can be married to many women at the same time. Mohammed is said to have had between 9 and 14 wives, the exact number is not clear.

Prostitutes Fulfill Many Roles

3) Prostitutes can make the world safer for women and healthy for normal men. Rather than encourage rape, or sexual harassment from sexually frustrated men, prostitutes are there for people who have a strong sex drive and cannot find anyone to have sex with or who enjoy sexual variety. For the socially inept man, they cope with all those with confused and repressed sexuality, removing the risk of attack they cause to other women. But most clients are just ordinary, normal men, your neighbors, the man in the Church pew next to you, your children's teacher, your lawyer, or politician. Some of us well adjusted normal men enjoy physical intimacy with a variety of women and it is physically and emotionally healthy for otherwise healthy men.

4) Prostitutes become experts who can offer high-quality sex. If there was not such a negative stigma, most everyone would want to visit prostitutes for erotic inspiration and self-indulgence. They provide the chance for new experiences without entering a new relationship, which many people find of enormous value at certain stages of their lives. In some cul-

tures, it is customary for all young men to learn about sex from the local prostitutes before they have sex with other women.

5) Prostitution is the oldest profession and should be respected. Like any other profession, there are the experts, the specialists, the all-rounders, the scoundrels and the bad people who need hounding out. Bad people such as the cash-and-dash scams ruin the reputation of the industry as do those few that are on drugs, drink too much or just think of men as ATM machines.

6) Prostitutes offer many services often far more than just sex. Prostitutes call themselves all kinds of names, from whore to therapist; slut to Tantric teacher; hostess to surrogate. Each have their own style but when you listen to what they actually do, most provide approximately the same range of services. They act as listeners (to everyone in pain, including sufferers of child sexual abuse), pacifiers (often of the same), substitute mothers, sisters and brothers, they enact fantasies, dominate to force those who are normally in control in their work and social lives to play submissive; whores may also play sub[missive].

Prostitutes fulfill all kinds of roles: from a quick hand-job behind a carrier bag in the park, to dinner and all night bed companion to "girlfriend" for a month's holiday.

Some do this with grace and love, others with one eye on the clock and the other eye on his wallet, hoping to steal it. There are sex workers who can actually adapt their mindsets to "fall in love" with each client, in order to give them maximum benefit of the time spent. There are others who despise all clients and play tricks to make them come fast. But there are many who sincerely love and enjoy men, and for them it is an ideal profession and not only about men as ATM machines. These are usually the most successful sexworkers since men can tell their sincere enjoyment of what they do.

A Satisfying Job

7) It can be a satisfying job. The fact is that a growing number of women are switching to work in sex rather than in other jobs because they find it gives them more freedom and job satisfaction. You choose your hours, you make more money per hour than most of your friends and you spend your time giving pleasure (and often receiving it too).

Some women who may once have opted for a career in nursing find it more satisfying offering a caring "hands on" service caring for people's personal needs. So many people in society have never been touched caringly or had their emotional needs catered [to]. Sex work allows caring individuals to offer such services, and they often just advertise as a prostitute because this is the easiest way to make a living.

8) Many men need teaching. Sociologists recognize that many men pay for sexual gratification and emotional solace because they have not yet learned to find either elsewhere. Many shy, socially phobic and disabled men rely on prostitutes to teach them how to gain a positive body image, seduce and make love. The book *Shadow Syndromes* by John J. Ratey and Catherine Johnson identifies a high incidence of minor forms of Aspergers Syndrome in males in Western cultures, which means that they can't respond to normal invitations of emotional bonding and socialization.

9) Prostitution enables many women to liberate themselves. It is not uncommon for women to enter the sex industry in order to establish their own sexual identity. . . . There are many situations where women decide to enter sex work because it seems to be the only way they can throw their sexual repressive background to the wall. They usually have to keep quiet about it and never identify themselves publicly.

10) Prostitution provides a better alternative to starving or stealing. When a woman is desperate to feed herself and her children and has no other income, prostitution is often the best option for her. One woman is quoted as saying that work-

ing as a street worker to provide the money to buy heroin for herself and her partner is better than him going out thieving because he might get a long prison sentence. (McKeganey, Neil and Barnard, Marina *Sex Work on the Streets* [1996]). But there should be safe off-street in-calls available or zones of tolerance so as to not be a public nuisance "in the face" of the public in neighborhoods where not wanted. If prostitutes want respect they should also respect neighborhoods and businesses that do not want street hookers in front of their homes or businesses.

11) Prostitutes educate. Prostitutes provide a service where people can learn. A young person can learn about their orientation and how to become a good lover. A couple can experiment with group sex. Isolated people can learn how to become intimate, people can learn about S/M [sadomasochism] and explore their submissive or dominant sides.

12) Prostitutes provide fun. They offer a service of pleasure. In countries where women are allowed to work together, there are clubs where people go along for an orgy: sex parties with several prostitutes and a group of clients. People enjoy visiting prostitutes for light-hearted yet intensely erotic experiences, which may be very difficult to find elsewhere.

13) Prostitution is good for mental health. Comforting sex without ties is excellent for mental health, soothing the nervous system, and helping the client improve their sense of well being.

14) Prostitution can cure problems. People with social disabilities such as stammerers can be helped to overcome their problems by loving attention and uncovering anxieties. People who have been sexually abused as children often need a lot of patient body work to overcome sexual difficulties, and prostitutes are invaluable in this work.

15) Sex work can be empowering. People gain personal strength from selling their bodies because their clients worship and admire them, they have as much sex as they want

and they defy traditional mores and roles imposed on them. Often prostitutes are extremely healthy, playful, creative, adventurous and independent women.

CHAPTER 3

What Policies Should Govern Prostitution?

Prostitution Should Be Legalized

Economist

In the following article the editors of the Economist, *a British newsmagazine, discuss how attitudes have changed about prostitution. The editors note that in the past, many governments tolerated prostitution, but due to the globalization of sex trafficking (that is, foreign prostitutes in local red-light districts), puritans have convinced policy makers that any form of prostitution is intolerable. Instead of cracking down on prostitution, as the puritans demand, the* Economist *argues that legalization is the best way to control it. Legalization would give prostitutes access to health care, brothels would develop reputations they would take pains to protect, and sex trafficking and other abuses could be more easily tackled. The editors conclude that sex between strangers harms no one and the government should stay out of the transaction.*

Two adults enter a room, agree [on] a price, and have sex. Has either committed a crime? Common sense suggests not: sex is not illegal in itself, and the fact that money has changed hands does not turn a private act into a social menace. If both parties consent, it is hard to see how either is a victim. But prostitution has rarely been treated as just another transaction, or even as a run-of-the-mill crime: the oldest profession is also the oldest pretext for outraged moralising and unrealistic lawmaking devised by man.

In recent years, governments have tended to bother with prostitution only when it threatened public order. Most countries (including Britain and America) have well-worn laws against touting on street corners, against the more brazen type of brothel and against pimping. This has never been ideal, partly because sellers of sex feel the force of law more strongly than do buyers, and partly because anti-soliciting statutes create perverse incentives. On some occasions, magistrates who have fined streetwalkers have been asked to wait a few days so that the necessary money can be earned.

So there is perennial discussion of reforming prostitution laws. During the 1990s, the talk was all of liberalisation. Now the wind is blowing the other way. In 1999, Sweden criminalised the buying of sex. France then cracked down on soliciting and outlawed commercial sex with vulnerable women—a category that includes pregnant women. Britain began to enforce new laws against kerb-crawling earlier this year [2004], and is now considering more restrictive legislation. Outside a few pragmatic enclaves, attitudes are hardening. Whereas, ten years ago, the discussion was mostly about how to manage prostitution and make it less harmful, the aim now is to find ways to stamp it out.

The puritans have the whip hand not because they can prove that tough laws will make life better for women, but because they have convinced governments that prostitution is intolerable by its very nature. What has tipped the balance is the globalisation of the sex business.

The White Slave Trade

It is not surprising that many of the rich world's prostitutes are foreigners. Immigrants have a particularly hard time finding jobs that pay well; local language skills are not prized in the sex trade; prostitutes often prefer to work outside their home town. But the free movement of labour is as controversial in the sex trade as in any other business. Wherever they work, foreign prostitutes are accused of driving down prices, touting "extra" services and consorting with organised criminal pimps who are often foreigners, too. The fact that a very small proportion of women are trafficked—forced into prostitution against their will—has been used to discredit all foreigners in the trade, and by extension (since many sellers of sex are indeed foreign) all prostitutes.

Abolitionists make three arguments. From the right comes the argument that the sex trade is plain wrong, and that, by condoning it, society demeans itself. Liberals (such as this newspaper) who believe that what consenting adults do in private is their own business reject that line.

From the left comes the argument that all prostitutes are victims. Its proponents cite studies that show high rates of sexual abuse and drug taking among employees. To which there are two answers. First, those studies are biased: they tend to be carried out by staff at drop-in centres and by the police, who tend to see the most troubled streetwalkers. Taking their clients as representative of all prostitutes is like assessing the state of marriage by sampling shelters for battered women. Second, the association between prostitution and drug addiction does not mean that one causes the other: drug addicts, like others, may go into prostitution just because it's a good way of making a decent living if you can't think too clearly.

A third, more plausible, argument focuses on the association between prostitution and all sorts of other nastinesses, such as drug addiction, organised crime, trafficking and underage sex. To encourage prostitution, goes the line, is to encourage those other undesirables; to crack down on prostitution is to discourage them.

Brothels with Brands

Plausible, but wrong. Criminalisation forces prostitution into the underworld. Legalisation would bring it into the open, where abuses such as trafficking and under-age prostitution can be more easily tackled. Brothels would develop reputations worth protecting. Access to health care would improve—an urgent need, given that so many prostitutes come from diseased parts of the world. Abuses such as child or forced prostitution should be treated as the crimes they are, and not discussed as though they were simply extreme forms of the sex trade, which is how opponents of prostitution and, recently, the governments of Britain and America have described them.

Puritans argue that where laws have been liberalised—in, for instance, the Netherlands, Germany and Australia—the new regimes have not lived up to claims that they would wipe out pimping and sever the links between prostitution and organised crime. Certainly, those links persist; but that's because, thanks to concessions to the opponents of liberalisation, the changes did not go far enough. Prostitutes were made to register, which many understandably didn't want to do. Not surprisingly, illicit brothels continued to thrive.

If those quasi-liberal experiments have not lived up to their proponents' expectations, they have also failed to fulfil their detractors' greatest fears. They do not seem to have led to outbreaks of disease or under-age sex, nor to a proliferation of street prostitution, nor to a wider collapse in local morals.

Which brings us back to that discreet transaction between two people in private. If there's no evidence that it harms others, then the state should let them get on with it. People should be allowed to buy and sell whatever they like, including their own bodies. Prostitution may be a grubby business, but it's not the government's.

Prostitution Should Be Decriminalized

Wendy McElroy

Wendy McElroy is the author of XXX: A Woman's Right to Pornography *and has written many other books and magazine articles. In the following essay she compares liberal and radical feminist views of prostitution. Liberal feminists defend prostitution as a woman's right to control her own body, while radical feminists believe that prostitution is an act of violence against women. McElroy supports the liberal feminist view of abolishing all laws that prohibit the buying and selling of sex. She maintains that laws against prostitution are used to harass and oppress women, while ignoring their male customers and pimps. Only decriminalizing prostitution will give prostitutes the same protection any other woman expects.*

Different societies have viewed prostitution in widely divergent ways. Some cultures stoned whores to death. In ancient Greece, however, prostitutes were an integral part of religious rites. In Napoleonic France, courtesans were educated and talented women. They were not simply respected: they were adored and often eagerly sought out as wives. Other societies have grudgingly tolerated prostitution as a safeguard for the family. It was deemed to prevent rape and to shield virtuous wives from the unsavory sexual appetites of their husbands.

The feminist movement has also expressed different opinions on the issue of prostitution. The pioneering 18th century British feminist Mary Wollstonecraft considered street prostitution to be a more honest pursuit than marriage, which she called 'legal prostitution.' Over a century later, the American

Wendy McElroy, "An Overview of 'Solution' to Prostitution." www.zetetics.com. Reproduced by permission.

socialist feminist Emma Goldman maintained "it is merely a question of degree whether [a woman] sells herself to one man, in or out of marriage, or to many men."

Still other 19th century feminists, who were involved in the purity crusades that characterized the Progressive Era, vilified prostitution. In her essay "Not Repeating History," the contemporary advocate for prostitutes' rights Gail Pheterson reflects on the advice offered by Josephine Butler. Butler was a 19th century British radical who championed the rights of prostitutes:

> In 1897, Butler warned her political associates ". . .beware of purity workers (who are). . .ready to accept and endorse any amount of coercive and degrading treatment of their fellow creatures in the fatuous belief that you can oblige human beings to be moral by force."

The Modern Feminist Debate

Controversy over the issue of prostitution has clouded feminist movements throughout history. It is a controversy that often reveals more about the ideology of the movement at that time—or of a faction within the movement—than it does about prostitution itself. The modern debate reveals deep and fundamental ideological conflicts.

Liberal feminism is divided on the issue. Old-fashioned liberals, who remember the slogan "a woman's body, a woman's right," tend to favor prostitutes' rights. Still riding the wave of tolerance that swept the '60s and '70s, these liberals tend to view prostitution as a victimless crime: that is, an activity in which all parties are consenting adults, an activity that is a crime only because it offends the moral sensibilities of uninvolved and uninjured third parties. Some liberals carry tolerance one step farther into advocacy. They defend prostitution as an extension of the right of consenting adults to perform whatever sexual acts they wish.

Individualist feminists, arguing from the principle of self-ownership, also advocate the rights of prostitutes. To them, prostitution is the reverse of rape during which a woman's body is taken without her consent. In prostitution, a woman fully consents to sex and often initiates it. If society respects a woman's right to say "no" to sex, they argue that society must also respect her right to say "yes."

There is a difference, of course, between prostitution and straight consensual sex. Prostitution is not merely an exchange of sexual favors; it is a financial exchange. At this point, individualist feminists rise to defend the free market as well as a woman's self-ownership. This is expressed by the question: "Prostitution is a combination of sex and the free market. Which one are you against?"

Both '60s liberal and individualist feminism view prostitutes as women in control of their own sexuality. . . that is, prostitutes set the price, the timing and circumstances of the sexual exchange. So what's the problem? Isn't [essayist] Camille Paglia correct when she states "the prostitute is not, as feminists claim, the victim of men, but rather their conqueror. . . ."?

Blaming Patriarchal Society

Paglia sees the real problem with prostitution arising from the hypocrisy and double standards of society. The current second-class citizen status of prostitutes is a reflection of American Puritanism more than anything inherent in the profession. Our society tells women to "marry well", to get things from men, and to use flirtation to gain favors. Advertising presents sex as a commodity, as part of the medium of exchange. Prostitution is just the logical extension of this societal attitude. But, because prostitutes flagrantly reveal attitudes that are usually left unstated, they are reviled.

To a point, gender (or radical) feminists agree: society is to blame, not the prostitutes. More specifically, male-dominated society—as expressed through capitalism and patriarchy—is to blame. But this realization does not sway them toward advocating the rights of prostitutes. Quite the contrary. Gender feminists seek to eliminate the oldest profession because it is a creation of patriarchy and, thus, an inherent act of violence against women as a class.

In her essay, "Prostitution in Contemporary American Society," [sociologist] JoAnn L. Miller explains how a seemingly voluntary exchange is actually an act of force:

> Prostitution involves one gender's taking advantage of its superior social status and manipulating the other gender. . . Because members of this less powerful group are compelled or forced, physically or psychologically, to engage in a sexual act, prostitution is fundamentally coercive and exploitative.

Prostitution, it is claimed, legitimizes the social attitudes that subjugate women as a class. Thus, prostitutes have a moral and political obligation to stop selling their bodies because these transactions fortify the cultural assumptions that damage women. These assumptions are said to have dire consequences. Specifically, prostitution is said to lead to rape. Thus, prostitutes are contributing to the rape culture.

In her pioneering book *Against Our Will* [feminist] Susan Brownmiller insists:

> The case against toleration of prostitution [is] central to the fight against rape, and if it angers a large part of the liberal population to be so informed, then I would question in turn the political understanding of such liberals and their true concern for the rights of women.

What Should Be the Legal Status of Prostitution?

The starting point of any debate should be to define the key terms of the discussion so that everyone understands what is being said. The key terms of this particular debate are "abolition," "legalization," and "decriminalization."

1. Abolition (or suppression): government attempts to prohibit all acts of prostitution, as well as the activities that promote it, such as keeping a brothel. Abolition—or absolute criminalization—is often considered to be the extreme opposite of legalizing prostitution. Actually, it is the ultimate in state control of that profession. Abolitionists call for all forms of prostitution to be considered a criminal offense and suppressed by force of law.

2. Legalization (or regulation): government has registered prostitutes with the police and subjected them to rules meant to protect health and public decency. Legalization refers to some form of state-controlled prostitution. It often includes mandatory medical exams, special taxes, licensing, or the creation of red light districts. It always includes a government record of who is a prostitute, information which is commonly used for other government purposes. For example, some countries in Europe indicate whether a person is a prostitute on his or her passport. This restricts that person's ability to travel since many countries will automatically refuse entry on that basis. Controlling legalized prostitution usually falls to the police.

3. Decriminalization (or tolerance): all laws against prostitution have been abolished. It refers to the removal of all laws against prostitution, including laws against pimping. Almost all prostitutes' rights groups in North America call for the decriminalization of consensual adult sex on the grounds that laws against such sex violate civil liberties, such as the freedom of association.

Why Prostitution Should Be Decriminalized

The individualist feminist approach to prostitution is to advocate decriminalization: that is, the abolition of all laws against selling sex. There are several reasons for this:

1. Laws against prostitution have historically been used to harass and oppress women in the sex industry, not the men

who are customers. This means that laws against prostitution almost amount to *de facto* [in practice] laws against women.

Even laws against pimps (assumed to be men) add to the persecution of prostitutes. This is because pimping is defined in economic terms; a pimp is merely an associate of a prostitute who receives any of her earnings. It has nothing to do with whether or not the woman is forced to perform sex. This definition of a pimp is so broad it includes roommates, lovers, male adult children, and friends. The associates of prostitutes are often rounded up under the charge of pimping. This violates the prostitute's right of free association.

Moreover, since pimps are almost defined as "those habitually in the company of prostitutes", anti-pimping laws interfere with the prostitute's right to marry. A husband would automatically open himself up to charges of pimping.

Prostitution Laws Are Laws Against Women

2. Laws against activities associated with prostitution also become *de facto* laws against women. For example, laws against running a brothel. . . In 1949, the General Assembly of the United Nations adopted a legal guideline, ostensibly meant to protect prostitutes. The document entitled "Convention for the Suppression of the Traffic in Persons and of the Exploitation of the Prostitution of Others." It read, in part:

> The parties to the present convention further agree to punish any person who:
>
> Keeps or manages, or knowingly finances or takes part in the financing of a brothel;
>
> Knowingly lets or rents a building or other place or any part thereof for the purpose of the prostitution of others.

Such laws effectively deny prostitutes the right to work indoors in a warm, safe, and clean place. They also make it difficult for women to band together for safety because those

[who] work in tandem could be charged with running a brothel. Anti-brothel laws make prostitutes isolated and vulnerable.

3. Anti-prostitution laws ensure that prostitutes will be unable to report violence committed against them to the police. Because the complaints come from criminals, they are next to never taken seriously or pursued. Even the murder of a prostitute is often ignored. On the contrary, prostitutes who complain to the police are likely to be further abused. Margo St. James claims that 20% of violence against prostitutes comes from pimps, 20% from police, and 60% from clients. . . about whom prostitutes cannot go to the police.

Prostitutes receive no protection from the state, even though they give a fortune to it by paying off fines.

4. Criminalizing prostitution has driven the profession underground and resulted in horrible working conditions for the women involved. Moreover, its black market nature attracts other illegal activities to the trade. This, in turn, creates a vicious cycle. For example, the stigma and awful working conditions of prostitution drive women toward drugs, which are then cited as a reason to strengthen laws against prostitution. Yet drug addiction is a problem that can be linked to many professions, not the least of all the medical profession. Only in the case of prostitution are laws enacted against the profession itself.

Censorship Against Women

5. Anti-prostitution laws function as a form of censorship against women, because they keep prostitutes from speaking up for fear of being targeted by police. In Europe, for example, many countries stamp the passports of prostitutes to identify them as such. Other countries may refuse to admit them. This serves to restrict the prostitute's travel and activities.

To avoid being branded, prostitutes lie about what they do and keep silent. Speaking out might result in losing custody of their children and opening up lovers and friends to charges of pimping. In some countries, everything a prostitute owns can be taken away from her as the proceeds of illegal activity. Such repression also hinders the ability of prostitutes to organize politically.

6. To the extent that prostitution creates a public nuisance, laws already exist to prevent these problems. The most commonly cited public nuisances include: children may have to walk by prostitutes and, so, suffer psychological trauma; prostitutes may destroy the image and safety of a neighborhood; they cause noise and fights during the night; non-prostitutes may be more vulnerable to harassment due to the presence of whores.

Smoke Screens

Feminists should realize that public nuisance arguments for anti-prostitutes laws are smoke screens. These laws are not aimed at removing a nuisance—namely, what prostitutes do, e.g., cause noise or disturbances. They are aimed at removing what prostitutes *are* —women who sell sex. This is clear from the many anti-prostitute ordinances that require no evidence of bad behavior for a charge to be brought. After all, any real nuisance that a prostitute creates could be dealt with under existing public order laws that make it illegal to publicly hurl threats, abuse or obscenity. The purpose of anti-prostitution laws is to target a specific category of women for persecution.

As for straight women who are afraid to be out at night. . . the real problem lies not with the prostitutes, but with the men who harass and/or physically abuse *any* category of woman. Male violence cannot be blamed on prostitutes, any more than domestic violence can be blamed on wives.

If gender feminists are concerned with the safety and dignity of women, they should join hands with prostitutes and help them to walk out of the shadows in which they now live and work. They should cease to feel sorry for prostitutes and start talking to them as equals. Feminists need the insights of prostitutes as much as prostitutes need the political clout of feminists.

Feminists of all stripes should speak with one voice to demand the safety of these women by granting them the same protection as any other woman can expect. Only decriminalization can provide this.

Legalization and Decriminalization of Prostitution Would Not Help Prostitutes

Angela N. White

Angela N. White says that prostitution is about control over women's bodies, and in the following essay she examines liberal and radical feminist views about who has control of the prostitute's body—the prostitute or the man who purchases her services. This disagreement over control extends to the areas of legalization and decriminalization. White contends that legalization gives the state permanent control of prostitutes and therefore does not make prostitution less demeaning. White also asserts that decriminalization would not benefit prostitutes because they would remain virtual prisoners of their pimps, nor will it end the practice of illegal prostitution. Prostitution can be eradicated, but only when women are convinced they have choices other than prostitution and when their customers and pimps are subjected to more severe punishments, she claims. White is an editor for American Jurist, *a publication of American University's Washington College of Law.*

Crack whores. Wild West brothels. High-class escorts. Julia Roberts. Prostitution can bring different and conflicting images to the minds of those who likely never have met a prostitute. Whether we're beating up "street hookers" in video games, worshipping self-proclaimed pimps like Ice-T and Kid Rock, or incarcerating prostitutes for what many would call a "victimless" crime, we obviously have little respect for these women.

Angela N. White, "Prostitution: A Crime Against Prostitutes," *American Jurist*, March 1, 2003. Reproduced by permission.

But prostitution isn't a victimless crime, and prostitutes aren't called "women." They're whores, tramps, sluts, pieces of meat—names for what society perceives as less than human. Despite the reasoning behind anti-prostitution laws, we are not the victims of prostitution in need of protection. The victims are those who, under the current law, are punished for the very crimes committed against them.

Is Prostitution a Choice?

Many agree that the criminalization of prostitution does not accomplish its supposed intent. Prostitution has hardly been slowed, much less stopped, but a rift exists on the anti-criminalization side of this debate. The breaking point is the definition of prostitution: Is it a valid means of income that a woman can and should freely choose for herself, or is it sexual slavery no matter how willingly the woman seems to have entered the profession?

Those who advocate prostitution as simply another job think of prostitutes as individuals who rationally considered the alternatives and chose prostitution over other means of making an income. Prostitution advocates assume much in determining this. They assume that women, absent coercion or drug addiction, can choose the type of prostitution they wish to practice. There is a hierarchy to prostitution. The escorts and call girls we see in movies-of-the-week do exist, and they can live extravagant lifestyles with minimum risk of abuse or arrest. This is hardly how most prostitutes operate, however. Activist prostitutes in particular argue from an elitist viewpoint that they should have the right to do as they wish with their bodies without considering those who do not have similar opportunities. This type of prostitute is blind to the plight suffered by many of her "colleagues." She cannot grasp that a prostitute who can write and publish an article about her profession is, in reality, in a class above most prostitutes.

Prostitution proponents tend to work from the viewpoint of liberal feminism—men and women start out on a level playing field, and any law that doesn't keep the field level is discriminatory. Proponents believe that laws criminalizing prostitution unfairly discriminate against women, who make up the majority of prostitutes. Many liberal feminists treat the right to prostitution as they do the right to abortion—women's bodies, women's choice. But prostitution and abortion are not so similar. Abortion involves women gaining control over their bodies. Prostitution involves men purchasing control over women's bodies.

This is the view held by many prostitution opponents. Unlike liberal feminism, radical feminism identifies women as an oppressed class. Under this view, there is no equal playing field—if left unchecked, patriarchy will favor the rights of men at the expense of women. As with pornography, radical feminists find themselves linked at the hip with their usual enemy, the Religious Right, on this issue. But instead of fearing social corruption and the Four Horsemen of the Apocalypse, many radical feminists see prostitution as a form of sexual slavery and a human rights violation.

To radical feminists, prostitution is not a "choice." Studies consistently place the average age of girls entering prostitution to be in the early teens. Many prostitutes were sexually abused as children and escaped the violence by running away from home. A Toronto study once found that 90 percent of prostitutes questioned wanted to get out of prostitution but felt they could not. The presence of pimps, who control the actions of prostitutes and take most, if not all, of their profits, contribute to this belief. Feminist scholar Catharine MacKinnon even proposed that prostitutes sue pimps and johns under the Thirteenth Amendment for indentured servitude.

Can We Rid Society of Prostitution?

The criminalization of prostitution has its roots in Victorianism—prostitution was seen as morally wrong from a religious standpoint, but nonetheless a necessary evil to keep men's "uncontrollable" desires from being taken out on "respectable" women. Hence, prostitutes were not considered to be in the same sphere as these women, and eventually not in the category of women at all. This attitude prevails today, justifying the belief that prostitution will always exist in some form.

Radical feminists don't buy this attitude. Cities spend millions of dollars each year to arrest and incarcerate prostitutes—money that could instead be used for education, job training, housing, and counseling. If fewer women felt that they have no choice but to sell their bodies to survive, the supply necessary to sustain prostitution would diminish.

Prostitution—a Man's Crime

One must wonder, however, if eliminating prostitution is, in fact, the goal. Prostitution is often more about control than about sex. The ability to purchase a woman's body gives men affirmation of the power they have in our society. No matter how powerful they may already be—CEOs, politicians, judges—purchasing a prostitute allures many of them.

Prostitutes, especially those working on the streets, are the most raped of any class of woman. They are regularly raped by clients, pimps and policemen. Clients also hold power over prostitutes through the ability to pay (or not to pay). Pimps hold the power to intimidate while appearing to care for and coddle their victims, a talent they share with abusive husbands and boyfriends.

Society is responding to ineffective anti-prostitution laws by making the penalties more strict, but typically only for the prostitutes. Texas went so far as to pass a three-strikes law in 2001 making a third conviction of prostitution a felony. Technically, working on the "level playing field" theory, most states have adopted laws that allow the equal punishment of prostitutes and johns. But police and courts hardly enforce these laws equally. In many states, prostitutes make up the majority of participants who are arrested, whereas johns are typically given a citation. Johns who are arrested are less likely than prostitutes to be convicted, and when arrested, are more likely to be fined instead of incarcerated.

If eliminating prostitution were the goal, the government would focus on rehabilitating current prostitutes, as well as preventing future ones. Those who make the laws seem to have no desire to stop the pool of women who become trapped in prostitution. Men benefit from this never-ending supply of desperation.

An issue distinct from why prostitution shouldn't be criminalized is how it should be treated. Legalizing prostitution allows the government to control the types of prostitution allowed and to enforce health and zoning regulations. Decriminalizing prostitution removes all laws against it, essentially making it a laissez-faire business.

Nevada—How Legalization Can Go Wrong

Nevada is the only state to have legalized prostitution, and only a few counties in the state have actually done so. Prostitution, solicitation, pandering and living from the earnings of a prostitute are still illegal in Nevada, but an exception is made for prostitution that occurs in a licensed brothel.

Many have called the governments of these counties pimps, and rightly so. Laws vary depending on the county, but women in these brothels usually must work 14-hour days, seven days a week, for three weeks straight. They have no control over who their clients are and must give a reason considered satisfactory by the brothel management to refuse a customer. The prostitute must give up approximately half of her earnings to management. They are often not allowed to leave the brothel except under limited circumstances. Many counties do not allow the prostitute to live or socialize in the same area where she works.

Mandatory health checks are the most commonly touted advantage to legalizing prostitution. They also can cause the most problems for the prostitute. While the prostitute is tested regularly for HIV and other STDs [sexually transmitted diseases], their clients are typically not tested beforehand. Once a prostitute has become infected by one of these untested johns, her career is over. Because the requirement to register with her local government also causes her to indirectly register with the FBI, her chances of getting another legal job or health insurance for her new disease are slim.

Legal prostitutes in Nevada are not even given the decency of being treated as employees. Instead, they are considered independent contractors, allowing the brothel management to fail to provide them with insurance, pension or retirement.

Why Complete Decriminalization Hurts Women

The goal of decriminalizing prostitution should not be to make it easier for women to enter and continue in the profession. Prostitution will not become less demeaning to women when it is legal. We can rid ourselves of this crime against humanity, despite what we have been told, if we are committed. We must not only cut the supply of prostitutes through educational and other social programs, but also cut the demand. Laws against pimps and johns should not be abolished, but strengthened. They are the true antagonists in this piece.

Decriminalizing all crimes associated with prostitution will do nothing for the prostitutes who are held as virtual prisoners by their pimps. And it will do nothing to stop the purchase and abuse of women's bodies. In order for prostitution to cease, our laws must recognize that prostitutes are not criminals, but are a class of people in need of protection.

Cities Are Using Humiliation Tactics to Fight Prostitution

Amanda Paulson

In the following article Amanda Paulson, a reporter for the Christian Science Monitor, *writes about the city of Chicago's attempt to crack down on prostitution by publicizing the names and photos of the men who are arrested for soliciting prostitutes. In addition to having their photos posted online, the arrested must attend an eight-hour "john school" where they learn about the law, the health risks of patronizing prostitutes, and the daily lives of prostitutes. City officials hope that these measures will deter men from purchasing prostitutes' services, Paulson says.*

Anyone who's ever wondered just who the men are who cruise [Chicago's] seedier strips looking for sex can now satisfy their curiosity.

Starting in [June 2005], the Chicago Police Department has been posting the names of "johns" arrested for engaging or soliciting prostitutes—along with their photo, address, age, and place of arrest. A recent sample included men from low-income Chicago neighborhoods and relatively well-to-do suburbs, of all ages and ethnicities.

Cracking Down on Demand

It's part of a tactic more and more cities are using, cracking down on prostitution by focusing on demand, often using tactics of humiliation—like Chicago's website or billboards in Oakland, Calif.—to try and convince potential customers to stay home.

It's a trend that some applaud, saying the men who drive the trade have been overlooked too often while prostitutes get arrested. Others question its effectiveness, suggesting that websites and "john schools" that educate customers about the realities of prostitution accomplish little.

"The first thing you have to ask is why are people involved in prostitution—overwhelmingly it's related to economic issues," says Juhu Thukral, director of the Sex Workers Project at the Urban Justice Center in New York. Focusing on demand, Thukral says, won't reduce the amount of prostitution; rather, more resources should go toward supportive housing, job training, and legal services—"programs that teach people how to get mainstream jobs that will provide a living wage."

Still, others involved in the issue say that efforts like Chicago's are an encouraging sign that cities are both waking up to the problems around prostitution and are recognizing that customers play as important a role as the prostitutes.

In Chicago, the website has been up for only a month, but has gotten more than 497,000 hits, says David Bayless, a spokesperson for the Chicago Police Department.

"If we can get them to think twice about coming here, if they think they're at risk of being arrested and having their picture online, then the website's done its job," he says. "It's an acknowledgment that customers are contributors to the problem."

"John" School

In addition to getting their photo online and having their vehicle impounded, arrested men have to attend a local "john school" run by Genesis House, an organization that helps Chicago sex workers.

The men pay $500 to attend the eight-hour class, and the money goes to support Genesis House's programs. During the day, they learn about the law, the health risks of patronizing prostitutes, and the reality of what life is like for prostitutes.

"This is not a victimless crime," says Patti Buffington, director of Genesis House. "There is a victim here, and it's the women performing this. About 95 percent of these woman were abused."

For the men who attend john school, the biggest impact often comes when they learn more about the women themselves, says Norma Hotaling, a former prostitute who founded The Sage Project in San Francisco and started the nation's first john school about 10 years ago.

Midway through the class, she often reveals her own background. "You see them turn to Jell-O," Ms. Hotaling says with a laugh. "They say, 'You're smart, and you have power here, but you're a prostitute.'"

She's helped numerous cities around the US, including Chicago, launch their own john schools, and says the programs are remarkably successful; in San Francisco, she only sees about two percent of the men a second time.

Hotaling also has sympathy for the men who come through her classes; most, she says, simply don't have all the facts to make good decisions. As a result, she's not a fan of humiliation tactics.

"You don't tear down their support system and humiliate them," she says. "Do you want them to be total outcasts?"

Advocates at the Sex Workers Outreach Project, a San Francisco organization that favors legalizing prostitution, have also been outspoken against the humiliation efforts, such as the new campaign in Oakland that has billboards springing up with customers' faces—blurred in early versions—saying "Don't John in Oakland." "It's not going to stop the problem," says Robyn Few, director of the Sex Workers Outreach Project. "It's just going to move the problem from one place to another."

Just One Part of the Overall Effort

Still, many advocates of the efforts say the crackdown on customers is just one piece of an overall effort to reduce street prostitution and help sex workers move on to other jobs. In Chicago, where police estimate the number of prostitutes at anywhere between 16,000 and 25,000, Mayor Richard Daley has jumped with vigor on the new initiative. He cites not just the harm prostitution wreaks on neighborhoods and their quality of life, but also the harm done to the prostitutes themselves—a sign that politicians are starting to look at sex workers as victims rather than simply criminals.

"Once they become prostitutes, they're subject to even more violence, abuse, and possible death from their pimps and their customers," Daley said at a press conference to announce the new Internet site. "It's a terrible life, and a caring society has a responsibility to help these women turn their lives around, and to keep other young women from entering the profession."

Cities That Use Humiliation Tactics to Fight Prostitution May Violate Civil Rights

Tresa Baldas

In the following selection Tresa Baldas examines the decision by cities to post on their police Web sites the names and photos of men arrested for soliciting prostitutes. Civil rights activists claim that the practice punishes the men before they are tried in a court of law. City officials defend their actions by claiming that the men's names and photos are a matter of public record and can legally be viewed by anyone. In order to avoid potential liability, however, some cities post only the names and faces of those who have been convicted of soliciting prostitutes. Baldas is a staff reporter for the National Law Journal.

Chicago's use of the Internet to humiliate customers of prostitutes, or "johns," has led to concerns that the practice may violate constitutional rights.

At issue is Chicago's [2005] decision to run a Web site that posts the names and photos of people who have been arrested for soliciting a prostitute—but not convicted.

Attorneys and law enforcement officials argue that the practice violates a person's constitutional right to a fair trial, and could lead to lawsuits down the road.

The arguments whirling around in the Windy City have also taken place in cities in Kansas, North Carolina and Ohio. In Oakland, blurred faces of men arrested for soliciting a prostitute are being placed on billboards.

"Clearly it's punishment before judgment. How could it not be? It causes humiliation for the arrestee, his friends and

Tresa Baldas, "Cities' Practice of Shaming 'Johns' Raises Rights Issues," *The Recorder*, July 29, 2005. Reproduced by permission.

family . . . and they're all being punished without any hint of due process," said attorney Jack King, director of public affairs of the National Association of Criminal Defense Lawyers. "The city of Chicago is opening itself up to a lot of potential liability."

But Mayor Richard Daley has brushed aside potential constitutional concerns about the Web site, asserting that the public's right to know outweighs an arrestee's disapproval.

"It's a matter of public record," Daley spokesman David Bayless said of the mugshots that are posted on the Internet. "We're also responding to a demand from the media and the public to see who the individuals are." The Daley administration also has asserted that prostitution is "a terrible life" that subjects women to violence and abuse and jeopardizes the safety of neighborhoods.

Police Lt. Rick Edwards, of the Akron, Ohio, Police Department, which has a similar shame Web site, disagrees. "You're innocent until proven guilty. You could really bury somebody," noted Edwards, whose police department runs an "Operation John Be Gone" Web site that features only those convicted of prostitution charges.

Warnings Included

According to Daley's office, Chicago police [in 2004] arrested 3,204 prostitutes and 950 customers, and impounded 862 cars.

Hoping to cut the demand for prostitution, the city is also distributing posters, warning potential customers about the Web site and adding that "you will be paying thousands of dollars in fines for your public humiliation."

A similar public shame program was introduced in Kansas City, Mo., in the 1990s, where the police posted the images of people arrested on prostitution charges on a community-access TV channel.

Like Chicago, Kansas City also didn't wait for a conviction to run the photographs.

Kansas City Police Sgt. Brad Dumit defended the tactic, saying "it's a matter of public record and anyone can view it." The program ended due to a manpower shortage, he said. But in its four years of existence, he said, the city never ran into any legal troubles.

"We never had a problem with it whatsoever," Dumit said. "And I'm imagining Chicago's pretty smart. They won't be violating people's rights."

Charlotte, N.C., also has an off-again-on-again program called "Shame TV," which runs the names and faces of convicted "johns."

In Oakland in May [2005], 20 billboards went up on bus stops along the International Boulevard corridor at the request of City Council President Ignacio De La Fuente.

The four faces on each billboard are blurred, a fact the city's legal staff believes will protect Oakland from invasion-of-privacy claims. But that may change, said De La Fuente aide Carlos Plazola.

"The next set of billboards, according to my boss, will be billboards that will actually show real faces," Plazola said. "[But] the response was really contingent on the effect of this campaign. . . . At this point, things look pretty calm."

100,000 'Hits'

Publicizing the names of suspects was also debated a few years ago, but the city decided to name only those convicted, "for obvious reasons," noted Julie Hill, a spokesperson for the city of Charlotte.

Edwards said Akron's prostitution Web site got more than 100,000 Internet hits in the last year. Attorneys often try to keep their client's name off the Web site, seeking more jail time or a higher fine.

"They try to use the Web site as a bargaining tool and we don't bargain with it," Edwards said. "If you're guilty, you're going on the Web site."

Chicago Public Defender Darlene Williams, who handles prostitution misdemeanors for the Cook County public defender's office, said she is opposed to Chicago's humiliation tactic.

"You're putting people's pictures out there on a Web site and there isn't a presumption of innocence," Williams said. "They might not be convicted of anything and now there's this picture on this Web site and there's this humiliation brought to their family."

CHAPTER 4

Personal Views of Prostitution

Prostitution Is a Job Like Any Other

Jean Hillabold

Jean Hillabold is an instructor of English at the University of Regina, Saskatchewan, Canada. In the following article she writes about how she fell on hard times while she was in college earning her master's degree. None of her support systems was able to help her get back on her feet, so she took a job as an escort call girl to earn money. Hillabold recounts how going to work as an escort was much like going to work at any other job in which she was expected to please her male clients and bosses. And, she writes, it was also similar to going on a first date with men who expected sex, except this time she was paid cash in advance. She never experienced any violence while she was a prostitute; in fact, the men she feared the most were government workers—law enforcement, court officials, and those in academia—who could threaten her livelihood, her schooling, and who could take away her daughter. When her escort agency was raided, Hillabold worked intermittently as an escort for a few regular clients. But after she earned her degree and was offered a teaching job, she left prostitution behind for good.

"Executive Escorts Wanted." The ad in the classified section of the Regina *Leader-Post* was vague and euphemistic. The word "executive" didn't fool me into believing that sex work was glamorous, or that it would lead to a high-status career—on the contrary. I dialed the number and asked for the man who had placed the ad because I needed money.

Like most women who enter the sex biz at some point in their lives, I had not planned a career as a Scarlet Woman. In my twenties, I had assumed that an ability to type, file and serve the public could always get me an office job if nothing better was available. As a bride, I had assumed that if all else failed and my marriage ended, the legal system would force my husband to help provide for any children we might have, if not for me. As a graduate student, I had assumed that I could complete a thesis in a year or two, and then re-enter the job market with a Master's degree.

A Collapse of All Support Systems

When I turned 30 in 1981, I was facing the collapse of everything I had counted on. Advances in office technology had dried up the jobs that had supported me through my first college degree, and I didn't understand computers. As a divorced mother, I was told that I was entitled to child support, which my ex-husband refused to pay. His claim that he could not afford it seemed to satisfy the legal system. As a graduate student, I learned that I had few rights, if any. As my advisor continued to put off reading my latest chapter, I was repeatedly warned that I could be dropped from the program for failure to complete my thesis within the time allowed.

I "came out" as a lesbian and met a woman in the gay bar. While I was pressuring her to find a job and control her drinking, she rebelled by stealing the contents of my bank account. My only option was to apply for welfare, but I was told that I was not eligible as long as I still had the savings that I had locked into a Guaranteed Investment Certificate. I was terrified of being left without a cent.

Success at anything seemed beyond my reach. What more did I have to lose?

I responded to the escort ad. The pimp who asked me to meet him for an interview had a colourful history: he had sold dope of various kinds, including heroin (on which he was hooked), repossessed furniture and played pool for big prize money. He was running an escort agency as an economic sideline, and he seemed to be looking for women who understood what they were getting into. The euphemisms used in the newspaper and on the phone with strangers were largely intended to protect him and his "girls" from arrest. Sex was part of the interview, which did not surprise me. Like other employers, my new pimp explained the basic rules: safety on the job (the regular use of condoms plus medical checkups), honesty, reliability, appropriate dress (tight skirts, not ragged jeans). We had a deal.

Similar to Other Jobs

In some ways, going to work at my pimp's house at noon and leaving at five o'clock with cash in hand was different from anything else I had ever done. In other ways, this job was remarkably similar to jobs in which I had been expected to please male clients and supervisors who patted and patronized me because I was a "girl." Working as an escort also resembled going out with men who expected sex on the first date— except that, in this case, they paid in cash. In advance.

I was nervous every time I went alone to a hotel or a private home to meet a new john. I knew from experience that any woman can be perceived as "asking for" male violence. Luckily, I never experienced violence while doing sex work.

However, johns or even pimps were never the men I feared most. My fear of "the system" (government, police, the courts, even academia and the mental-health system) at this time is the hardest thing to explain to those who have not been in my shoes. All I can say to those who believe that all the major institutions of our society exist to serve the needs of the ordinary citizen (regardless of gender, race and class) is: it ain't necessarily so.

I knew that an undercover cop could legally arrest me (after enjoying the service he had paid for) for the "crime" of supporting myself and my child. I also knew that my ex-husband (who had confined me to our home for days at a time) was not considered "violent" by his friends, and that if he found out about my current job, he could probably win custody of our daughter. I knew that I would have little credibility with anyone outside the sex biz if I were abused in any way on the job.

My pimp, a man of few words who seemed to move in slow motion, turned out to be very reliable in his way. At the end of a working day he would come home, where I was usually alone in his house. (Most of his stable worked the night shift.) He would offer me a drink, and he seemed impressed that I never helped myself in his absence. He would ask about my day, and I would tell him how many "calls" I had had. Then he would ask for an agency fee for each call, or (more often) he would invite me into his bedroom to collect his "fee" in trade. I knew that my feminist friends would probably consider this a worst-case example of sexual exploitation, but it enabled me to keep every penny I earned. Since part of my job was to answer the phone, my pimp told me that he liked having me there in the daytime, and wanted to make sure I made enough money . . . and with a day job I could work on my thesis between calls and my daughter could attend childcare.

The story of my life in the "oldest profession" has several endings. My job with my first escort agency ended peacefully when my pimp told all his "girls" that he had sold his business—which essentially consisted of us—to a woman he knew who never contacted us. We assumed that she had her own stable, or preferred to find one herself. Years later, I heard that he had died of a heroin overdose. Wherever he is now, I wish him well. He might have been the only man I've ever known who never lied to me.

The Second Agency

One of my sister-escorts found a job with another agency and introduced me to the owner, a man from Newfoundland with two complete sets of identification. This time I worked nights.

PROSTITUTES REQUIRED

At Monica's

The oldest profession in town is now a 'legal profession'. Due to our increased popularity Monica's which is housed downstairs at The White House, is looking for more ladies to join the day & night shifts. Our very successful group of ladies of all ages, sizes and nationalities will make you feel right at home.

No experience? No problem! Our caring female management will teach you everything you need to know to enable you to become a successful Escort and Masseuse. Monica's Escorts have a fantastic reputation and our luxurious premises has ideal sensual decor and surroundings.

Fantastic Money, Fantastic Staff, Fantastic Conditions!

Stop wondering, don't hesitate any longer just pick up the phone and

CALL US TODAY - PERMANENT & TEMPORARY POSITIONS ARE AVAILABLE

Phone: 377 4343 and we'll answer all of your questions.

Applicants must be 18 years of age and over.

In Auckland, New Zealand, where prostitution is legal, the job of prostitute is respectable enough to warrant a want ad in a local newspaper in July 2003. © Dean Purcell/Getty Images.

I didn't realize that the police were watching the agency for several reasons: my pimp and his American wife, who worked along with the rest of us, were raising a toddler in the same house from which they ran their business, one of the other "girls" was wanted for armed robbery in another province, another was underage, and the owner of another agency was complaining that my pimp owed him money.

Now that I had more contact with other call girls, I learned more about the business I was in. All of us were single mothers. Several of us had grown up in middle-class families. Several of my co-workers seemed to be high on something most of the time. Most of them claimed to have strict limits on what they would do with a john, but no one excluded oral sex because it was in great demand.

As far as I could see, there was no big cultural gap between call girls and street workers. One of my "sisters" claimed to have worked the street for seven years before "taking a break" by joining an agency. She said that street work was more dangerous but also more fun in some ways, since hopping in and out of cars was fast and easy.

Despite the widespread belief of my older johns that all prostitutes were lesbians and vice versa, I found little overlap of those two communities. Most of my co-workers seemed so homophobic that I was relieved to find one who was also attracted to women, and I had a brief affair with her. Later on, I realized how little we had in common, but at the time, it was comforting to have a sexual relationship outside of "work" with someone who would not reject me because of what I did for a living.

The End of a Career

My job ended dramatically on April Fool's Day, 1984. While a lonely, divorced john kept me out all night, the police arrived at my pimp's house to round up everyone there. The next day, my girlfriend told me the news but assured me that we were small fish to the cops, who were more interested in shutting down our agency than in throwing us all in jail.

For better or worse, I owned the car that our pimp had been using for agency business, and I was told to go to the police station to claim it. I was questioned about the agency and was told that I would not be charged if I cooperated. My pimp was charged with several offenses, but he left town with his wife and child before he was due to appear in court.

For several weeks, I survived without the fast cash that could be gained from sex work. Then I was phoned by one of my regulars, a married john with grown children who were older than I was. He had asked one of my "sisters" for my home phone number, and she had given it to him. I told him that I was no longer in the business, and told him not to call me again.

The man called me from time to time, and I repeated the same message. Then he called when I needed money and I agreed to see him one last time. After that, my only john phoned me approximately every two weeks and eventually I took the risk of letting him visit me at home. The money I earned from him helped me over lean periods as I lurched from one temporary job to another.

In 1989, my thesis was accepted, I passed my oral exam (no pun intended), and graduated with a Master's degree. I refused to see my john any more, but after a five-year relationship (so to speak), he did not take my "no" seriously. With help from a new girlfriend who was on good terms with the police, I was able to stop the man from stalking me. He was warned that he could be charged under a new anti-stalking law. My career in the sex biz was finally over.

Eventually, I was offered a higher and more secure income in academia than I ever made as a call girl. Even if I could go back to my old life at my present age, I would not be tempted. Living in relative safety and comfort just feels too good to give up. Does this mean that I am a reformed prostitute who has climbed back onto the straight and narrow path? You be the judge.

Life with an Abusive Pimp

Tina Frundt

The following selection is from testimony given by Tina Frundt to a U.S. House of Representatives subcommittee that was holding hearings about sex trafficking. Frundt is a street outreach specialist for the Polaris Project, an organization based in Washington, D.C., and Tokyo, Japan, that combats trafficking in people. As an outreach worker, Frundt meets many girls with experiences similar to hers, when she was a prostitute working the streets. Frundt describes how she came to be a street prostitute and the abuse she suffered at the hands of her pimp. Frundt says her pimp told her she had to earn a minimum of five hundred dollars per night. When she did not meet her quota, her pimp would beat her and send her back out on the streets until she had the money. Frundt's pimp trained her through more abuse and intimidation to blame herself for her injuries. There was no one to help her, and so she accepted and became numb to the abuse.

I want you to think about the women and children that you have seen late at night, when you may be coming home from work or a social event. Maybe you have seen women in the streets in short dresses. You turn your heads to look away. We don't look at the faces of these young women and girls who are forced to be out in the street. Maybe we think this is what they want to do or they wouldn't be out there.

Living a Dream

I'm going to take you back 15–20 years ago, in Chicago, IL, when I was forced to be on the streets at the age of 14. When I was 14, I ran away from home to be with a "wonderful guy I

Tina Frundt, testimony before the House Subcommittee on Domestic and International Monetary Policy, Trade, and Technology, Committee on Financial Services, April 28, 2005.

met" that was in his mid-20's. We had a great plan about us living together, making money together, and becoming rich. I thought this was everything I had always wanted, until he told me that if I loved him, I would help make money for us. By the time I thought I was in love with him, he had given me too much to go back home. I was then introduced to the other women that he was pimping, who I hadn't known about before. That's what happens with pimps—at first, it's just you and them, but then there were four of us.

We went to Cleveland, OH, and he immediately said that I was going to go "out" with the 3 other women, so they could show me how to make money for "us," "for all of us together," as if we were like a family. Later on that evening, his friends that he knew came by the motel. At first he told me to have sex with one of them, and I didn't want to, so his friends raped me. Afterwards, he said "that wouldn't have happened if I would have just listened to him at first." So I took it as my fault. Instead of being angry at him for being raped, I was angry at myself for not listening to him in the first place. Right after that is when he picked my clothes out, told me what to wear, and forced me to go out on the streets.

Learning My Lesson

When I first went out into the streets, and I had to meet my first John, I felt like this was something I didn't want to do. I walked around the streets back and forth for hours, hiding, until the morning. Our quota was $500 but I had only made $50 that night to give back to the pimp. So he beat me in front of the other girls and made me go outside until I had made the money. This is the same man that took me out to eat, listened to me when I wanted to complain about my parents, and gave me words of advice, but increasingly, I was seeing a side of him that I had never seen before—a brutal side, where he repeatedly hit me in front of the other girls to show us all a lesson. Not only was I shocked, I was scared. What would happen to me if I did try to leave, and who would believe me if I told them that this was going on? So I worked from 6am until 10pm that next night, without eating or sleeping. I came back with the $500, but in his mind, I still hadn't learned my lesson. So I had to go back outside until 5 A.M. the next morning. After the second day, he finally bought me something to eat, but as a punishment to never to do it again he locked me in the closet to sleep.

Pimps are sadistic. They train you. Since that first night, I've been locked in the closet on numerous occasions, had my arm broken with a bat, and had my finger broken, which has never set right. After the abuse, the pimp would tell me to sit on his lap and ask me what was wrong. When I said, "You broke my arm," he hit me, and asked me again what was wrong. I had to say, "I fell down." No one else helped me. They just said I shouldn't have upset him, which helped teach me to blame myself. I wasn't allowed to see a doctor, so after my finger was broken, I just wrapped it with some tape.

Deaf Ears

This did not just happen to me when I was 14. It first started when I was 10 years old, in the foster care system, when I was abused by my foster mother's boyfriend. For money, he forced me and my foster brother, who was 13 years old, to have sex with men. When I tried to get assistance with social workers and let them know what was going on, it fell upon deaf ears. This brings us to the question of who is listening when our children are talking? Do we choose not to believe things because it's too hard for us to believe it's true and it's easier to ignore the problem? Or would it force us to realize that something needs to be done to the foster care system? The women and children we have come into contact with have started out on the streets at the age of 12–14, either by kidnapping [by] the pimp, forced into prostitution by a family member, or in the foster care system by foster parents.

What happened to me 15–20 years ago is still going on today. The young girls and women that we work with at Polaris Project are still going through the same things or worse than what I went through when I was young. Girls as young as 12 years old have to have sex 7 days a week, 365 days a year, usually from 10 P.M.–5 A.M. On an average night, they have sex with 10–15 people and have to meet a quota which is usually $500–1,000 a night. The young girls and women never keep their money. Who are you going to talk to about the abuse? After awhile, you become numb to the abuse. It happens to you so much, it's just like eating breakfast in the morning. You may not like what you eat but you get used to the routine.

Sold into Sex Slavery

Anita Sharma Bhattari

In the following testimony to a U.S. House of Representatives subcommittee during hearings on sex trafficking, Anita Sharma Bhattarai, a victim of sex trafficking, tells her story of being kidnapped and forced into prostitution. She says that while living in her native land of Nepal she boarded a bus and was befriended by a couple seated next to her. Unbeknownst to her, the couple drugged her, and when she woke up she was in India. She tells how the couple tricked her into going to a brothel where she discovered she had been sold into prostitution and had to earn money to buy her freedom. Bhattari says when she refused to work, she was beaten, and when she tried to escape, she was captured and brought back. Eventually she managed to escape and was taken in by an international justice organization.

My name is Anita Sharma Bhattarai. I am twenty-eight years old. I am from Nepal.

In [1998], my husband took another wife. Soon after, he began to beat me, torment me, and disregard my children. I decided it would be best if I and my children moved out of our home in order to support myself and my children.

I made money by buying vegetables from farmers and selling them in the village market. On November 22, [1998,] I boarded the bus in order to go pay for my vegetables. I sat next to a Nepali man and woman. They offered me a banana to eat and I took it. Soon after I ate the banana, while I was still on the bus, I got a very bad headache. I told the man and woman that I had a headache and they offered me a pill and a bottle of mineral water to help me swallow the medicine. Immediately, I felt myself becoming groggy and then I fell unconscious.

Anita Sharma Bhattarai, testimony before the House Subcommittee on International Operations and Human Rights, Committee on International Relations, September 14, 1999.

Taken to India

The next thing that I remember is waking up in the train station in Gorakhpur, India. I am from a mountain village. I did not know what a train was and, of course, I had never been to India. I asked the man where I was. I was confused by the long cars that I was riding in and the strange surroundings.

The man told me not to cry out. He informed me that there were drugs (hashish) tied around my waist and that I had just smuggled them across an international border. He told me that if I brought the attention of the police, I would be in trouble for smuggling the drugs. I did not remember the drugs being tied around my waist but I could feel plastic bags on my stomach under my dress.

The man also told me that if I stayed with him, I would receive 20,000 rupees from the sale of the drugs when we arrived in Bombay. I did not know how to get back to Nepal, I do not speak any of the Indian languages, and I believed that I was already in trouble for carrying drugs. The man told me that he was my friend and that I could refer to him as my brother. I decided to stay with him. It was a five-day journey to Bombay by train.

When we got to Bombay, he told me to wait at the train station while he went to sell the drugs. When he returned, he told me that the police had confiscated his drugs and that he did not have any money. He said that I would have to go to his friend's house and wait while he got some money. He called his friend on the phone from the train station, and she came to meet us there. She was a Nepali woman. She said her name was Renu Lama.

Tricked

I left the train station with Renu Lama. My "brother" told me that he would meet me at her house at 4 o'clock that afternoon.

As I walked with Renu Lama, she told me not to look at people because she lived in a very dangerous neighborhood and there were some bad people that I should not make eye contact with. When we arrived at her house, Renu Lama told me that I should take a bath. I told her that I would wait until 4:00 when my "brother" came because he was carrying my clothes. She told me my "brother" was not coming. I waited until evening but he never came. Finally, I took a bath and Renu Lama gave me some of her old clothes to wear.

Renu Lama then asked me if I could write a letter for her. I did. She dictated what she wanted to say to her family, and I wrote the letter. When I had finished writing the letter, Renu Lama took away the ink pen. She went to my room and took away all of the pens, pencils, and paper that I could possibly write with. I realized that the writing of the letter had been a test. Now that they knew I was literate, they were keen to keep me from communicating with anyone outside.

I felt very scared that evening and I refused to eat anything. I soon noticed that many men were coming in and out of the house and I realized that it was a brothel. I began howling and shouting. I said that I wanted to leave.

Renu Lama told me that I was ignorant. She said that I did not just come easily and I could not go easily. She said that I had been bought and I would have to work as a prostitute in order to pay them back. I was never told how much they had paid for me. Renu Lama and two of her associates told me that all the women in the house were "sisters" and that we had to support each other. I cried a lot, but they comforted me and brought me a fine dinner—complete with chutney and a pickle.

Forced to Stay

The next day, though, I insisted that I wanted to leave. The women began to slap me on the face. They cut off my hair. It was shoulder length in the back with short bangs in the front.

Now that I had short hair I knew that I could not leave the brothel without everyone identifying me as a prostitute. In my culture, short hair is the sign of a wild woman.

Then, I was told that all of the women in the brothel had to bathe three or four times each day. The women all bathe nude and they bathed together—four or five girls at a time. I had never bathed nude before and I had never bathed with other naked women. When I expressed my shyness, the other women mocked me. They grabbed me and stripped off my clothes. They forced me to bathe with them.

For the next couple of days the women beat me often. They slapped me on the face and head with their hands and hit me about the waist and thighs with metal rods. I begged to be let go. I said that I wanted to return to my children in time for the biggest holiday of our culture. The women mocked me. They told me that if I worked with them for a couple of days, they would send me home with three bricks of gold and 30–40,000 rupees for the festival.

I was also forced to learn Hindi—the language of most of the customers. At times [when] I couldn't speak enough Hindi, I was beaten about the waist and thighs with the iron rods.

When I was alone with one of the other women, I offered her my gold earring if she would let me go. She said no. Later I learned that three of the women were in the brothel voluntarily and they were in charge. There were six other women in the brothel and, I learned, they had all been tricked and forced like me. Renu Lama and the woman to whom I had offered my earring were in the brothel voluntarily.

All of the women in the brothel were from Nepal. The six who were forced had all been brought from Nepal but under different pretenses. One girl married a man [who] said he was taking her to Bombay to buy gold. He then left her in a brothel.

None of the other girls could read or write. I am literate because I am Brahmin and the women in my community are educated.

The women tried to reassure me that being a prostitute was not that bad. All of my food, housing, and clothes were provided. All I would have to do, they said, was sell my body.

Forced to Work

On the fourth day that I was in the brothel, my first client came to me. I refused to have sex with him. He had already paid for me so he grabbed me and tried to rape me. I fought him off. He had managed to get my clothes off but he was very frustrated because I was resisting him so much. He stormed out and asked for his money back. A couple of the brothel owners (voluntary prostitutes) came in and beat me. When they were done, the same man came back in. I then said that I would have sex with him only if he wore a condom. I knew about the need for condoms since I had learned that some of the other victims had very bad diseases. At first he refused but after another fight he finally agreed to wear a condom. By the time he left, he had used three condoms.

I only had one client my first day. But the next day, and everyday after, I had three or four clients each day. I managed to get an ink pen. I would write messages to the police on the inside of cigarette boxes and send them out with my clients. Many clients promised to help but none did.

Each client paid 220 rupees to be with me for an hour. I had to give the entire sum to the brothel owners. Often, the men would give me five or ten rupees extra. I used the money to buy condoms since the brothel owners would not provide them for me.

Still, I was not able to go out to buy the condoms myself. In fact, for the entire month and a half that I was in the brothel, I was never allowed to go out into the sun. Some of the other girls got to go the hospital when they fell ill. But I never got sick, so I could never leave.

I lived on the second floor of the brothel. The six of us who had been brought there against our will were kept on the second floor. There were no windows on our floor. The three who ran the brothel lived downstairs.

Downstairs there was a door that led outside. Several iron rods used for beatings leaned against the wall beside the door. One of the owners always guarded the door. Outside of the door was a metal gate. When customers were not coming in and out, the gate was closed. The gate was held by a heavy chain that was locked by a large padlock.

One night I tried to run away with one of my associates. We were caught by the brothel owners before we even made it to the gate. My friend was sold to another brothel in Sarat where the brothels are said to be even more tortuous than the ones in Colaba, Bombay, where I was held.

Escape

After serving clients for about eight days, an elderly man came to me as a client. When I was alone with him in the room, I told him that he was old enough to be my father. I told him, "I am like your daughter." I told him my story. He said that he had plenty of money and a Nepali friend. He promised to help me escape. He spent the entire night with me. That was the first time I had been with a client for more than an hour. I cried on him all night long.

The next morning he left with a promise that he would send his Nepali friend to help me. He said that I would know his friend had come when a Nepali man came to the brothel, asking to be with Anita, and carrying a gift of candies.

A few days later, a young Nepali man came to see me. He brought a gift of candy. I told him my story. He promised to help me escape. I told him that I did not trust anyone. In order for me to trust him, he would have to go to Nepal, report about me to my father and brother, and bring back some of my personal photographs as a result. The elderly client paid for him to go to Nepal. Before he left, the boy gave me his address in Bombay.

Some of my associates overheard the owners saying that they were also planning to sell me to a brothel in Sarat because I was too much trouble. I decided that I could not wait until the boy returned from Nepal. I had to try again to run away. I asked some of the other girls to run with me, but they were too afraid. We had been told that we would be killed if we tried to run away. But I determined that I would rather die than stay in the brothel. The other girls pooled their money together and came up with two hundred rupees. In exchange for the 200 rupees, I promised that if I made it out alive, I would get help for them. A couple of days later, I had a perfect opportunity. Renu Lama was out of town again. The owner who was watching the gate was drunk. A new maid had just been hired to clean and cook in the brothel. The new maid was doing chores and had left the gate open just a little bit. In the middle of the night, I would guess about 4 am, I ran out of the brothel. I was wearing only my nightgown and carrying a slip in my hand. I just ran down the street as fast as I could.

As I was running I saw two police officers. They were in civilian clothes but I knew they were police officers by the belts that they were wearing. I ran to them, told them my story, and handed them the address of the Nepali boy. They took 100 rupees from me in order to pay for a taxi. They put me in a taxi that took me to the Nepali boy's house.

When I arrived at the house, the Nepali boy was not there. But another Nepali man and his wife were there. They were friends of the Nepali boy and they agreed to take me in. The police left me with that family.

I did not know it at that time, but that same day, the Nepali boy had met Bob [Robert Mosier, Director of Investigations at the International Justice Mission]. He told Bob my story. Soon after I ran away from the brothel, Bob and the police raided the brothel where I had been. After searching through the brothel, the police with Bob learned that I had run away earlier that night. They came with Bob and met me at the house where I was staying.

Bob told me that I could go back to the brothel to get my things. I was too scared to go back because I thought I might be forced to be a prostitute again. But Bob assured me that I was safe. I went back to the brothel with Bob. I showed him all of the hiding places where they found the other girls. All of the girls who were forced [into prostitution] were released from the brothel and a way was provided for them to go back home. The two owners who were there that night are now in jail. Bob also arranged for me to return home to my family in Nepal.

Return to Nepal

First, I went home to my family but it was very uncomfortable. The people in the village laughed at me. In my culture, a woman is scorned if she is missing for just one night. I had been missing for two months. It was very hard for my family, especially since we are members of the Brahmin caste. So, today I live in Kathmandu. I work as a domestic servant in the city. I am still without my children since they went to live with their father when I was taken away. I am told that my husband's new wife is very cruel to my children. But my husband does not want my children to be with me because of where I have been.

I know that my story will help other women who are forced into prostitution. I am proud that I already was able to help Bob free the other girls in the brothel where I worked. Though I am grateful to be here to share my story, I am sad that I am not with my children—that my children cannot be here with me.

Organizations to Contact

Advocates for Youth
1025 Vermont Ave. NW, Ste. 200, Washington, DC 20005
(202) 347-5700 • fax: (202) 347-2263
e-mail: info@advocatesforyouth.org
Web site: www.advocatesforyouth.org

Advocates for Youth is the only national organization focusing solely on the prevention of pregnancy and HIV infection among young people. It provides information, education, and advocacy to youth-serving agencies and professionals, policy makers, and the media. It believes that child sexual abuse is a risk factor that could lead to prostitution. Among the organization's numerous publications is the brochure *Child Sexual Abuse: An Overview.*

Alan Guttmacher Institute
120 Wall St., New York, NY 10005
(212) 248-1111 • fax: (212) 248-1951
e-mail: info@agi-usa.org
Web site: www.agi-usa.org

The institute works to protect and expand the reproductive choices of all women and men. It strives to ensure that people have access to the information and services they need to exercise their rights and responsibilities concerning sexual activity, reproduction, and family planning. It considers laws enacted by the George W. Bush administration concerning sex trafficking and prostitution problematic as they impede efforts to fight HIV/AIDS. Among the institute's publications are the *Guttmacher Report*, *Family Planning Perspectives*, and *International Family Planning Perspectives*, which occasionally include articles on prostitution.

Captive Daughters
3500 Overland Ave., #110–108
  Los Angeles, CA 90034-5696
(310) 669-4400 • fax: (310) 815-9197
e-mail: captivedaughters@earthlink.net
Web site: www.captivedaughters.org

Captive Daughters was established to educate the public about
the extent and severity of the sex trafficking of women and
girls around the world. The organization believes that trafficking is a direct assault upon the human rights and lives of children and adolescent girls. Its goal is to end forced prostitution
of girls and women. Its Web site features many articles about
sex trafficking and child prostitution, including "Sex Trafficking of Children in San Diego," as well as an extensive resource
list.

Center for Women Policy Studies (CWPS)
1211 Connecticut Ave. NW, Ste. 312, Washington, DC 20036
(202) 872-1770 • fax: (202) 296-8962
e-mail: HN4066@handsnet.org
Web site: www.centerwomenpolicy.org

CWPS was the first national policy institute to focus specifically on issues affecting the social, legal, and economic status
of women. It is concerned with international trafficking of
women and girls into the United States for involuntary servitude and exploitation in a variety of settings, including sweat-
shops, brothels, domestic servitude, and farm work. Its available publications include fact sheets on violence against
women and girls and the report *Violence Against Women as
Bias-Motivated Hate Crime: Defining the Issues.*

Coalition Against Trafficking in Women (CATW)
PO Box 9338, North Amherst, MA 01059
fax: (413) 367-9262
e-mail: info@catwinternational.org
Web site: www.catwinternational.org

The Coalition Against Trafficking in Women promotes women's human rights by opposing sexual exploitation in all its forms, especially prostitution, trafficking in women and children, pornography, sex tourism, and mail-order bride selling. On its Web site are links to numerous articles about prostitution and sex trafficking, including "Sex Trafficking Is Not 'Sex Work,'" "Prostitution on Demand: Legalizing the Buyers as Sexual Consumers," and CATW's annual report.

Concerned Women for America (CWA)

370 L'Enfant Promenade SW, Ste. 800
  Washington, DC 20024
(202) 488-7000 • fax: (202) 488-0806
Web site: www.cwfa.org

CWA's purpose is to preserve, protect, and promote traditional Judeo-Christian values through education, legislative action, and other activities. It is concerned with creating an environment that is conducive to building strong families and raising healthy children. CWA publishes the monthly *Family Voice*, which periodically addresses such issues as prostitution and sex trafficking.

End Child Prostitution, Child Pornography, and the Trafficking of Children for Sexual Purpose (ECPAT-USA)

157 Montague St., Brooklyn, NY 11201
(718) 935-9192 • fax: (718) 935-9173
e-mail: info@ecpatusa.org
Web site: www.ecpatusa.org

ECPAT-USA conducts research on child sexual exploitation, including prostitution and trafficking, and conducts training sessions, raises awareness, and provides educational materials about human trafficking, child sex tourism, U.S. military involvement with child sexual exploitation, and child sexual exploitation in the United States. It also advocates for government policies and programs to prevent and end sexual exploitation of children. It provides fact sheets on commercial sexual exploitation of children, numerous papers about child prostitution and sex tours in different countries, and a quarterly newsletter.

Focus on the Family

8605 Explorer Dr., Colorado Springs, CO 80995
(719) 531-3400 • fax: (719) 548-4525
Web site: www.family.org

Focus on the Family promotes Christian values and strong family ties and campaigns against pornography, homosexual rights laws, prostitution, and sex trafficking. It publishes the monthly magazines *Focus on the Family* and *Focus on the Family Citizen* as well as the video *Sex, Lies, and . . . the Truth*, which encourages sexual abstinence and criticizes safe-sex methods, which its members believe increase the spread of AIDS. Publications available from its Web site include "Military Takes Aim at Prostitution."

The Heritage Foundation

214 Massachusetts Ave. NE, Washington, DC 20002-4999
(202) 546-4400 • fax: (202) 546-8328
e-mail: info@heritage.org
Web site: www.heritage.org

The Heritage Foundation is a conservative public policy research institute that supports the ideas of limited government and the free-market system. It promotes the view that the welfare system has contributed to the problems of illegitimacy and teenage pregnancy. Among the foundation's numerous publications is its Heritage Lecture Series, which includes "Freeing Women from Exploitation and Despair."

North American Task Force
on Prostitution (NATFP)

2785 Broadway, 4L, New York, NY 10025-2834
e-mail: prisjalex@earthlink.net
Web site: www.bayswan.org/NTFP.html

NATFP is an umbrella organization for prostitutes and prostitutes' rights organizations in the United States. Its goals are to repeal existing prostitution laws, promote the development of support services for sex workers, and end the stigma associated with prostitution. The task force strives to educate the public by distributing position papers, bibliographies, and other materials, and also provides speakers to lecture in college classes, at conferences and workshops, and in the media. It plans to begin an online library soon.

Office to Monitor and Combat Trafficking in Persons (G/TIP)
U.S. Department of State, Washington, DC 20520
(202) 647-4000
Web site: www.state.gov/g/tip

The Office to Monitor and Combat Trafficking in Persons coordinates U.S. government activities in the global fight against modern-day slavery, including forced labor and sexual exploitation. It helps coordinate antitrafficking efforts both domestically and around the world. G/TIP publishes the annual *Trafficking in Persons Report* and fact sheets such as "The Facts About Child Sex Tourism."

Polaris Project
PO Box 77892, Washington, DC 20013
(202) 547-7909 • fax: (202) 547-6654
Web site: www.polarisproject.org

The purpose of the Polaris Project is to combat human trafficking and slavery. Based in the United States and Japan, it brings together community members, survivors, and professionals to fight trafficking and slavery in the spirit of a modern-day Underground Railroad. Its Web site includes a selection of testimony from Polaris staff who testified before Congress, survivors of trafficking and slavery, and a fact sheet on human trafficking.

Prostitution Research & Education (PRE)
PO Box 16254, San Francisco, CA 94116-0254
(415) 922-4555
Web site: www.prostitutionresearch.com

Prostitution Research & Education opposes the institution of prostitution and advocates for alternatives to prostitution—including emotional and physical health care for women in prostitution. It develops research and educational programs to document the experiences of people in prostitution through research, public education, and arts projects. PRE's Web site includes links to articles about prostitution and sex trafficking, including "Prostitution, Violence, and Post-Traumatic Stress Disorder," "A Comparison of Pimps and Batterers," and "The Natasha Trade."

Sex Information and Education Council of the United States (SIECUS)
130 W. 42nd St., Ste. 350, New York, NY 10036
(212) 819-9770 • fax: (212) 819-9776
e-mail: siecus@aol.com
Web site: www.siecus.org

SIECUS is an organization of educators, physicians, social workers, and others who support an individual's right to acquire knowledge of sexuality and who encourage responsible sexual behavior. The council promotes comprehensive sex education for all children that includes AIDS education, teaching about homosexuality, and instruction about contraceptives and sexually transmitted diseases. Its publications include fact sheets, annotated bibliographies by topic, the booklet *Talk About Sex*, the bimonthly *SIECUS Report*, and the article "The Rights of Women in Prostitution."

Sex Worker Outreach Project (SWOP)
333 Valencia St., Ste. 445, San Francisco, CA 94103
Web site: www.swop-usa.org

SWOP focuses on improving the lives of sex industry workers by promoting safety and dignity in sex work and fostering an environment that affirms individual choices and occupational rights. SWOP spearheaded an initiative in Berkeley, California, to decriminalize prostitution. Its Web site includes links to prostitution articles from around the world.

Bibliography

Books

Alexa Albert · *Brothel: Mustang Ranch and Its Women.* New York: Ballantine, 2002.

Jeanette Angell · *Callgirl.* Sag Harbor, NY: Permanent Press, 2004.

Kevin Bales · *Disposable People: New Slavery in the Global Economy.* Berkeley and Los Angeles: University of California Press, 2004.

Karen Beeks and Delila Amir · *Trafficking and the Global Sex Industry.* Lanham, MD: Lexington, 2006.

Barbara Ehrenreich and Arlie Russell Hochschild, eds. · *Global Woman: Nannies, Maids, and Sex Workers in the New Economy.* New York: Metropolitan, 2003.

Melissa Farley, ed. · *Prostitution, Trafficking and Traumatic Stress.* Binghamton, NY: Haworth Maltreatment & Trauma Press, 2003.

Kathryn Farr · *Sex Trafficking: The Global Market in Women and Children.* New York: Worth, 2005.

Gary A. Haugen with Gregg Hunter · *Terrify No More: Young Girls Held Captive and the Daring Undercover Operation to Win Their Freedom.* Nashville: W. Publishing Group, 2005.

Victor Malarek — *The Natashas: Inside the New Global Sex Trade.* New York: Arcade, 2004.

Rachel Masika, ed. — *Gender, Trafficking, and Slavery.* Oxford: Oxfam, 2002.

Roger Matthews and Maggie O'Neill, eds. — *Prostitution.* Burlington, VT: Ashgate, 2003.

Paola Monzini, ed. — *Sex Traffic: Prostitution, Crime and Exploitation.* London: Zed, 2006.

Tracy Quan — *Diary of a Manhattan Call Girl.* New York: Crown, 2001.

Nils Johan Ringdal — *Love for Sale: A World History of Prostitution.* Trans. Richard Daly. New York: Grove, 2004.

John Geoffrey Scott — *How Modern Governments Made Prostitution a Social Problem: Creating a Responsible Prostitute Population.* Lewiston, NY: Edwin Mellen, 2005.

David Henry Sterry — *Chicken: Self-Portrait of a Young Man for Rent.* New York: Regan, 2002.

Isabel Vincent — *Bodies and Souls: The Tragic Plight of Three Jewish Women Forced into Prostitution in the Americas.* New York: William Morrow, 2005.

Rebecca Whisnant and Christine Stark, eds. — *Not for Sale: Feminists Resisting Prostitution and Pornography.* North Melbourne, Australia: Spinifex, 2004.

Periodicals

Nwando Achebe   "The Road to Italy: Nigerian Sex Workers at Home and Abroad," *Journal of Women's History*, Winter 2004.

John L. Allen Jr.   "Holland: Tolerance Fuels Social Experiment the Dutch Way," *National Catholic Reporter*, October 19, 2001.

Amber Arlene   "Could I Ever Forgive Him?" *Marriage Partnership*, Spring 2003.

Erin Gibbs van Brunschot   "Community Policing and 'John Schools,'" *Canadian Review of Sociology and Anthropology*, May 2003.

Bebe Moore Campbell   "One Sisterhood, Under God," *Essence*, November 2004.

Coalition Against Trafficking in Women   "Every Woman Has a Right Not to Be Prostituted," *Off Our Backs*, March 2001.

Lisa Takeuchi Cullen   "Teenage Wasteland," *Time International*, December 3, 2001.

Melissa Farley   "Prostitution Is Sexual Violence," *Psychiatric Times*, October 1, 2004.

John Gibb   "Hookers at Sports Day," *Spectator*, November 23, 2002.

Jan Goodwin   "Afghan Girls Forced to Sell Sex—or Starve," *Marie Claire*, April 2002.

Jan Goodwin   "Rescued from Hell," *Marie Claire*, July 2003.

Aina Hunter   "School for Johns," *Village Voice*, May 10, 2005.

Rick Jervis   "'Pleasure Marriages' Regain Popularity in Iraq," *USA Today*, May 4, 2005.

Kimberly Klinger "Prostitution, Humanism and a Woman's Choice," *Humanist*, January/February 2003.

Nicholas D. Kristof "Sex Slaves? Lock Up the Pimps," *New York Times*, January 29, 2005.

Phelim McAleer "Happy Hookers of Eastern Europe," *Spectator*, April 5, 2003.

Tara McKelvey "Of Human Bondage," *American Prospect*, November 2004.

Rebecca Mead "American Pimp: How to Make an Honest Living from the World's Oldest Profession," *New Yorker*, April 23, 2001.

Carol Mithers "Rescuing the World's Girls," *O: the Oprah Magazine*, November 2004.

Mireya Navarro "Long Silent, Oldest Profession Gets Vocal and Organized," *New York Times*, December 18, 2004.

William F. Nelson "Prostitution: A Community Solution Alternative," *Corrections Today*, October 2004.

Kelly Patricia O'Meara "Bush Taking Battle to the Sex Trade," *Insight on the News*, November 10, 2003.

Alex Perry and Mae Sai — "The Shame," *Time International*, February 4, 2002.

Leah Platt — "Regulating the Global Brothel," *American Prospect*, July 2, 2001.

Janice G. Raymond — "Sex Trafficking Is Not 'Sex Work,'" *Conscience*, Spring 2005.

Mian Ridge — "Massaging the Facts," *Spectator*, October 29, 2005.

Larry Rohter — "Prostitution Puts U.S. and Brazil at Odds on AIDS Policy," *New York Times*, July 24, 2005.

Sarah Schafer — "Not Just Another Pretty Face," *Newsweek International*, October 13, 2003.

Suzanne Smalley — "'This Could Be Your Kid,'" *Newsweek*, August 18, 2003.

Craig S. Smith — "Turkey's Growing Sex Trade Snares Many Slavic Women," *New York Times*, June 26, 2005.

Brandon Spun — "Closed Doors and Childhoods Lost," *Insight on the News*, January 28, 2002.

Martina E. Vandenburg — "Out of Bondage," *Recorder*, February 18, 2005.

Wendy Murray Zoba — "The Hidden Slavery," *Christianity Today*, November 2003.

Index